The Last Good Obsession

The Last Good Obsession

Thoughts on Finding Life in Fiction

SANDRA SWINBURNE

Judith Kitchen Select

OVENBIRD

Ovenbird Books, 2013
Port Townsend, WA

Ovenbird Books
Port Townsend, WA
Judith Kitchen Select

This book is published under the Judith Kitchen Select imprint of Ovenbird Books, a new publishing venture designed to bring literary nonfiction titles to the attention of the reading public. In the interest of quality and individuality, Judith Kitchen acts as editor and introduces each book; the writer has complete autonomy over content and design.

Author photograph: Andrew Swinburne

Ovenbird Books Nonfiction Series
With a forward by Judith Kitchen
www.ovenbirdbooks.org

Library of Congress Cataloging-in-Publication Data is on file.

ISBN 13: 9781940906027
ISBN: 1940906024
Library of Congress Control Number: 2013920015
CreateSpace Independent Publishing Platform
North Charleston, South Carolina

For Andy, Mathew, Ian, Nora, and Alec
And for those who are now gone, but remembered

Thanks to readers in the Rainier Writing Workshop at Pacific Lutheran University for thoughtful suggestions along the way, and to faculty reader Lia Purpura. Special gratitude to my mentors, Judith Kitchen and Stephen Corey.

To Maureen Brilla-Fitzpatrick who gave me permission to use *Behind Closed Doors*: Just this once it's okay to judge a book by its cover.

I'm pleased beyond measure to be included in the Judith Kitchen Select imprint of Ovenbird Books—and I add my voice to the ovenbird's call: "Teacher, teacher, teacher."

Contents

Behind Closed Doors: An Introduction   xi

On Reading Slant   1

For Sandra Love Frank McGuinness XX   13
    There Came a Gypsy Riding, Frank McGuinness
Sorrows and Silence   29
    Last Orders, Graham Swift
Vanishing Woman Seeks Adventure   49
    The Crying of Lot 49, Thomas Pynchon
Faulkner's Lover   63
    Light in August, William Faulkner
Perhaps the Last Time   83
    Identity, Milan Kundera
Living with Goodness   99
    Madame Bovary, Gustave Flaubert
Women and Love   111
    Women in Love, D. H. Lawrence
Hot Stuff   125
    Lolita, Vladimir Nabokov
Advancing the Plot   149
    Washington Square, Henry James

Sandra Swinburne

Miracles and Luck   169
   The End of the Affair, Graham Greene
After the Falling   187
   Falling Man, Don DeLillo
Readings and Notes   205

The Author   209

Behind Closed Doors: An Introduction

S andra Swinburne has found the perfect art for the cover of *The Last Good Obsession*. Inside the room—a domesticated room with a woman's certain touch—there is taste and order. But outside, oh, there is another world waiting. Careful, some clouds are wisping through the window, invading her carefully arranged life. And isn't that the perfect metaphor for what books do to Sandra Swinburne? "There we all are, living in fiction," she says—and a whole new way of reading comes into play.

The Last Good Obsession is a reader's feast, and Swinburne is a female Sven Birkerts in bringing us this rich response. I say "female" because, although she assesses and responds to books in Birkerts' fashion, she is also willing to be vulnerable to the emotions she encounters in herself. She takes the time to think about why a particular book offers her the time-warp of transformation. She invites a book to take her out of herself in order to lead back into herself. Allows for a little gossip, a little intimacy. A glimpse into the interior.

Swinburne's introduction alerts us to the pitfalls of theory, or at least the frustrations of trying to find a way to speak of what happens when you pick up a book and see yourself moving within its pages. For Swinburne, books are alive, not to be analyzed or synthesized, or anything-ized, but because the imagined characters can speak to, or for, us. They are more us than we are. So this life in reading unfolds, book by book, and through seeing Swinburne respond to character or author, we learn to know her life—not just her reading life, but the lived life she brings to her reading. Watch her worry about her choices, or ponder the long view necessary for a daughter, wife, parent. Watch her imagine a glass of wine with an author, or a fling with a character, and you will see how literature works its magic in the heart of a woman open to experience, whether it actually happened or not.

Swinburne not only lives in fiction, she makes a sweet nonfiction of showing us the way that happens. We re-read novels with her in order to see new meanings, but also to feel what she felt while reading, think what she thought. An almost triangular relationship is set up between author, character, and reader. In this case, though, the reader is doubled—Swinburne becomes a character for your reading attention.

Look again at the painting on the cover. You're in the reading world, and whether it's Graham Greene or Don DeLillo or Henry James, you may be caught in the author's gaze—but you're gazing back, penetrating the mind of the writer. How *can* you tell the dancer from the dance? You admit that you can't, and then you go through that door with Sandra Swinburne and begin the waltz of the mind. You can't put it down—the book of her reading—even as you pick up the threads of your own life mirrored in hers.

—Judith Kitchen, October 2013

On Reading Slant

I cannot always say clearly where
I stop and the fictional life begins.
—Sven Birkerts, *Readings*

I sometimes have my nails done, an occasional indulgence that began two years ago when my friend Mary talked me into going
with her—"For fun," she said. I still go to my original manicurist, a
young Vietnamese woman named Nancy who works to help support
her family. My justification for this small luxury is that I like Nancy
and want to give her my business. I'm also fascinated by her efficiency
as she clips and soaks and polishes my ridged nails into a state of artificial and indolent beauty. While watching her work, I always notice
that her own nails are short and unpainted—except for the tip of her
right thumb which is streaked with an assortment of colors picked up
from running that nail around stray dabs on customers' fingers.

During a recent appointment, Nancy immediately commented
that she had not seen me in a long time. I replied that I was no longer
teaching at the local community college, and didn't pay much attention to my nails while working at home. Nancy filled a small basin
with warm water, spread a white washcloth on her manicure table,
and selected her tools while I hung up my coat and studied the little
bottles of iridescent nail polish lining shallow plastic racks. I weighed
the visual effects of red, orange, pink, or mocha, and gauged the

emotional pull of names like New York Siren and Toast of the Town. I chose a sheer tint of pink and took my place in the waiting chair.

Nancy went to work on my hands and on making conversation with me—often taking up a parallel conversation in rapid-fire Vietnamese with her sister-in-law, who is also her employee. Part way through the manicure, Nancy asked me what I was doing at home all day and I clenched defensively: I didn't want her to think that, while she was chipping thick toenails and sanding calluses, I was lying on the couch looking at magazines and watching television. I said that I was writing, perhaps a book, but progress was slow. A volley of Vietnamese momentarily took me off the hook, but then Nancy re-engaged and asked what I was writing about. That's when things got tricky.

How could I say—without sounding as if I thought I were performing free-lance brain surgery—that each day I try to read and think and write about what it means to be alive? How could I explain that time slips away while I'm living in fiction and searching for my own mysterious self? I decided to keep it simple: "Well, I read books and then I try to write about what they do to me, how they make me feel."

Nancy looked up from her work on my nails, crinkled her nose, and asked, "Who cares?"

There I was, engaged in a real conversation about reading and writing, and I didn't have an answer to what sounded like a simple question. I shrugged a silent reply intended to mean "Beats me," and promptly changed the topic while absorbing the implications of having chosen a color called Hopelessly in Love. But as soon as I got home, I phoned my friend Mary and drew the whole scene at the salon for her viewing pleasure. Trying to recapture the tone of Nancy's voice, the absolute absence of guile, I repeated the unanswered question a few times: "Who cares? Who cares?" Mary and I laughed and I admitted that I didn't know; I just didn't know who might care—besides me.

The Last Good Obsession

I continued to pick at Nancy's question until frustration resulted in a mutation: *Why* do I care? *Why* do I care about what books do to me? I concluded that the subtle knot of reading and writing shapes my life, my woman's life, in important ways. When I inspect the list of books that matter to me, I see that many of them are classic novels written years before I was born, their stories so familiar to experienced lovers of literature that mention of their names can provoke a quick I-know-all-about-it response. But I openly admit to knowing not nearly enough about certain books, old or new, that feel mysteriously important to me.

I often re-read my favorites and try to write my way into understanding what they mean, what all the ideas they set loose mean— only to realize that, while immersed in fictional worlds, I bump into my own vulnerable self. There I am, struggling at every turn like a character in the story; and there they are, my failures and frailties, rising from the pages, never so obvious as when I see them paraded by a woman who was imagined into existence by an author, often a male author. Sometimes I encounter my family and friends creeping about between paper covers, and they, too, are revealed in new ways under new names. There we all are, living in fiction.

What if I try on the ways that male authors imagine women in their novels—presumably from having "read" the real women they have known—then burrow into those spaces where my lived life and literature converge, opening both at once? What about the buzz of gender tension that I feel while immersed in the work of a male author, and what about when I notice something that's not quite right? What about those times when I wonder what he would think of me? Why not risk a marriage of critical thoughts and personal feelings?

The reasons that those questions need asking can be fished out of a literary tradition chock full of power disparities; responding to literature in a subjective voice has been frowned upon by the Academy in the past, and still is among scholars and professional writers who choose to focus on what can be done to a book and author rather than what the book does to the reader. Those who treat texts as objects fastidiously avoid mention of their own feelings in their writing, and one of them can usually be counted on to say, "Criticism should be *criticism*." In the end, those who publish also influence.

As I reason my way into that absence of the human self in their reading and writing, I suspect some cling to objectivity from fear of being branded and dismissed with the *N* that stands for *narcissist*. But under the guise of objectivity, a pretentious demonstration of critical theory or a performance rooted in I'm-smarter-than-the-author can drip narcissism. Dark thoughts dart through my head when I read slick critical maneuvering that aims to challenge and defeat an author. I wonder: Are we so programmed to compete that we reflexively turn an engagement with a text into a contest of wits rather than an opportunity to see life illuminated? Are we so disconnected from each other and from the meaning of our lives that we've stopped thinking and writing about the trials and tenderness we experience every day, stopped noticing those very things in our literature?

Writers who mingle personal or memoir material with literary criticism face risks; the loss of restraint and indulgence of psychological needs that seem ridiculous (worse yet, boring) to readers can be the death of such a hybrid. The proverbial "fine line" applies to the distance between self-absorbed therapy in print and honest understanding that is brought to consciousness through literature. Yet, even when the balance tips in a mixture of personal and critical writing, the alchemy of book and self can result in a sort of glorious peril.

D. H. Lawrence wrote essays about reading that are sometimes brilliant, sometimes reprehensible, and consistently personal. In *Studies in Classic American Literature*, a collection published in 1923, he reveals more about himself than the books he is "studying." Criticizing Ben Franklin's list of moral virtues for good citizens, Lawrence asserts that in writing such lifeless drivel, "the snuff-coloured little trap" could only have been motivated by "sheer human cussedness," and living within such a "barbed wire corral" of rules will guarantee the absolute absence of rapture on earth. Lawrence accuses Americans—in their lives and their art—of embracing mechanized emptiness and forsaking the "wild life" within the soul of man. He exhibits his own passion as the best argument against intellectual efforts to mold an identity of contrived perfection: "The ideal self? Oh, but I have a strange and fugitive self shut out and howling like a wolf or a coyote under the ideal windows. See his red eyes in the dark? This is the self who is coming into his own."

While many of us thrill to the energy in that prose and enjoy a laugh at Old Ben's expense, feminist readers cannot help but see red in response to Lawrence's essay on Hawthorne and *The Scarlet Letter*. Fixated on Arthur Dimmesdale's loss of masculine authority to the "hell-cat" Hester Prynne, Lawrence indulges in a misogynistic rant as his anger and sexual anxieties pour forth: "A woman can use her sex in sheer malevolence and poison, while she is *behaving* as meek and good as gold. Dear darling, she is really snow-white in her blamelessness. And all the while she is using her sex as a she-devil, for the endless hurt of her man." Not satisfied with word-venom, he recommends taking action, regardless of the consequences: "Give her the great slap, just the same, just when she is being most angelic." Troubling as this subjective criticism is, I find myself guiltily fascinated by Lawrence and his tormented fantasies; I want to re-read Hawthorne's story and test my own response to the gender dynamics between Hester and Arthur.

Should the critical reader and writer simply resist giving voice to the unpredictable self that waits behind closed doors? I cannot help but wonder whether I. A. Richards thought of Lawrence when he devised a systematic program of corrections for what he regarded as wrong-headed reading. In his 1929 publication *Practical Criticism: A Study of Literary Judgment*, Richards complains that "poetry has not yet received half so much serious systematic study as the technique of pole-jumping," and proposes a disciplined method for reading verse that focuses on the actual text rather than external influences or subjective response.

Under a chapter title that carries clear warning, "Irrelevant Associations and Stock Responses," Richards diplomatically, but firmly, addresses what he regards as the problem of subjectivity:

> The personal situation of the reader inevitably (and within limits rightly) affects his reading, and many more are drawn to poetry in quest of some reflection of their latest emotional crisis than would admit. . . . The dangers are that the recollected feelings may overwhelm and distort the poem and that the reader may forget that the evocation of somewhat similar feelings is probably only a part of the poem's endeavour. It exists perhaps to *control and order* such feelings and to bring them into relation with other things, not merely to arouse them.

Richards' method fortified territorial beliefs that literary criticism belongs in the Academy and, according to M. H. Abrams, earned him a spot next to T. S. Eliot as a forefather of a textual approach that was to become known as the New Criticism movement. Successfully silencing subjective voices that opposed their impersonal manner, New Critics dominated English departments in America for decades. Abrams explains that during those years, the literary object, without genre distinction, was largely isolated from collateral influence; what mattered were "words, images, and symbols rather than character, thought, and plot."

Some eighty years after Richards helped steer literary criticism toward explication of words on the page, his influence prevails when scholars bristle in response to Camille Paglia's subjective, pop-culture-laced readings of the Western canon. In her introduction to *Break, Blow, Burn*, a collection of forty-three essays about specific poems, Paglia takes her stand: "Good writing comes from good reading. Humanists must set an example: all literary criticism should be accessible to the general reader. Criticism at its best is re-creative, not spirit-killing."

Shaped by New Criticism during her own education, Paglia acknowledges that systematic attention to the "paradox and ambiguity" of poetic language is irreplaceable. However, she finds that something is missing from strict adherence to that formalism: "The New Critics' admirable reaction against a prior era of bibliographic pedantry had eventually resulted in an annihilation of context, an orphaning of the text." Rather than work within an approach to literature that ignores living reality and specifically evades "the sex and aggression in artistic creativity," Paglia broke from theoretical confines.

In *Sexual Personae*, a study of art and decadence, Paglia explains her determination to dive into literature and get personal: "Behind every book is a certain person with a certain history. I can never know too much about that person and that history. Personality is western reality. It is a visible condensation of sex and psyche outside the realm of word."

Paglia's interest in individuality appealed to me since it follows that not only does the author leave a unique fingerprint on a book, each reader does, as well. But when she overplays the tenet that sex and aggression drive art just as "nature creates by violence and destruction," and leans too heavily on a style that can feel like confrontational, gender-based attitude—"The commonest violence in the world is childbirth, with its appalling pain and gore. Nature gives males infusions of hormones for dominance in order to hurl them against the paralyzing mystery of woman, from whom they would otherwise shrink"—she loses the ordinary readers she claims to serve. As I read more of *Sexual Personae*, I was disappointed to admit that Paglia's subjective energy fizzles under the weight of an agenda, a repetitive agenda.

Meanwhile, the "strange and fugitive self" described by Lawrence peers through the windows and I want to hear its howl. I read to be dazzled by all manners of beauty and brilliance and darkness that emanate from the minds of others, but I also read to find my own red-eyed self. Why not allow my mind to exist in fictional worlds for the pleasure of being there, for being surprised or even scared by what I find? And why not write about what I might discover? In *How to Read and Why*, Harold Bloom allows that a first reading of a novel may not result in immediate attachment and may even be "an exasperation"; but for whatever mysterious reasons, once a novel is yours, a repeat engagement "instructs you in what is deepest in your own yearnings." In contemplating reasons to read and re-read the alpha novel *Don Quixote*, Bloom asserts that "Cervantine figures" exist within many of us: "There are parts of yourself you will not know fully until you know, as well as you can, Don Quixote and Sancho Panza."

Lawrence Weschler's engagement with art, which he approaches as but one link in a world full of interrelationships, shows what a reader of pictures—or prose—can learn about being alive. In the essay "Vermeer in Bosnia," Weschler considers images of women in Vermeer's paintings that were long seen primarily as "moralizing genre images." He sees something else: "Vermeer deploys the conventional iconography precisely so as to upend it. No, his paintings all but cry out, this person is not to be seen as merely a type, a trope, an allegory. If she is standing in for anything, she is standing in for the condition of being a unique individual human being, worthy of our own unique individual response."

Here's what I want: I want to stand with those women—the women in the Vermeer paintings, Joanna Burden, Oedipa Maas, Emma Bovary, Dolores Haze, and countless others—who have been imagined into being so that we can look at each other, and be looked at. I want to feel the pulse behind my own impulse to read and write so that I can draw a woman's life—through them, through me—in the same way that artist David Hockney describes drawing "visual delights":

The Last Good Obsession

About sixty years ago, most educated people could draw in a quite skillful way. . . . Which meant they could tell other people about certain experiences in a certain way. Their visual delights could be expressed. . . . Today people don't draw very much. They use the camera. My point is, they're not truly, perhaps, expressing what it was they were looking at— what it was about it that delighted them—and how that delight forced them to make something of it, to share the experience, to make it vivid to somebody else. If the few skills that are need-ed in drawing are not treated seriously by everybody, eventually it will die. And then all that will be left is the photographic ideal which we believe too highly of.

Can't objective point of view and critical theory be compared to the metal frame and glass lens of the camera, artificial barriers that interfere with sensory immersion in what might live? A deep engagement with literature cannot be expressed without the reader/critic surrendering to the revelations and visceral delights within a fictional world.

But Hockney goes on to admit that photographs, juxtaposed, spliced, and joined as collage, began to fascinate him as a way to rep-resent the re-looking and the adjustments of perspective that the mind and the eye do naturally. He noticed that altered photographic views of a scene layered into the gazer's consciousness seem to overcome the absence of "time—lived time" that limits the impact of a single photograph. Through the subjective choices made in collage arrange-ments, Hockney infused technology-reliant art with his own head and heart; working with and through artificial barriers, he found himself able to enter truth sideways.

In the essay "True to Life: David Hockney's Photocollages," Weschler describes a defining moment in the effort to create human experience in art when Hockney discovers his own unanticipated presence in a photograph that he had taken: There he is, holding his camera, reflected in a mirror that hangs behind his subjects. After that serendipitous turn, Hockney purposely pushed living presence in art further with the inclusion of his own foot in a panel of views that scan Yosemite Falls—a sneaker-encased foot. And then both feet appear in collage images of the Grand Canyon because Hockney wants his audience (his reader) to *enter* the pictured world through him.

Weschler analyzes the presence of Hockney's feet in the collages and his remarks can be used to build an argument for a personal presence in literary criticism: "From this time on, Hockney usually included photographs of his own feet in the collages. In effect, his feet stood in for him; they planted him as they plant the presence of any subsequent viewer. Indeed, standing there, facing forward into the world before them, the world of vision, the feet seem transposed figures for the eyes themselves." But Weschler also observes that the subjects in Hockney's middle phase photo collage projects "don't quite live back at us." Hockney became obsessed with overcoming this "fixity," and began to interweave multiple moments and varied perspectives that would take the viewer/reader through experiences in the subjects' moving, living world.

Hockney himself offers a distillation of the meaning of art that speaks to my writing aspirations:

> Art is about correspondences—making connections with the world and to each other. It's about love in that sense—that is the basis of the truly erotic quality of art. We love to study images of the world, and especially images of people, our fellow-creatures. And the problem with abstraction, finally, is that it goes too far inward, the links become tenuous, or dissolve, and it becomes too hard to make those connections. You end up getting these claims by some of the formalist critics of the last few decades that art just isn't for everybody—but that's ridiculous.

The Last Good Obsession

So what about weaving together different perspectives while writing about reading? In relatively objective views, the woman who exists in fiction can be seen and heard as the individual she is in her author-fashioned world; but in positively subjective views, I can be found looking at her and looking at myself. Reading and re-reading over time allows the self to change, to garner different views, to layer experiences of fiction and reality through "lived time" in ways similar to David Hockney's approach to photo collage. Rather than flatly reject objective literary criticism, I can use a little, or skirt close to its edges as I create a sort of collage criticism. Perhaps the time is right for this sideways path toward personal and universal truths.

In spite of being unprepared to explain my life in literature to Nancy that day, I know that I will go on reading and re-reading books just as I have been. I'll enter fictional worlds and encounter ideas that seep into my mind where I can chip and sand them into something that feels beautiful and true. Why not test my woman's life against imagined possibilities? Why not look for meaning through writing essays that are at once critical *and* personal?

I also know that I will not limit myself to traveling in familiar places or taking up with easy truths. I want my ever-forming self to notice more and feel more of the old and the new. I want to read for what Harold Bloom predicts will happen: "Because you will be haunted by great visions: of Ishmael, escaped alone to tell us; of Oedipa Maas, cradling the old derelict in her arms; of Invisible Man, preparing to come up again, like Jonah, out of the whale's belly. All of them, on some of the higher frequencies, speak to and for you." *Listening to them, and listening to my own voice that rises from deep within, I form a plan: If I plant one foot in fiction and one foot in lived life, then invite others to join me in that way of seeing, perhaps we can "live back" at each other.*

For Sandra Love Frank McGuinness XX

"Lonely—it is, terrible to be lonely, talking to birds. Pitying snakes. Putting flowers at your door for bastarding St Patrick."
—Frank McGuinness, *There Came a Gypsy Riding*

I suppose it's possible that I'm not very discerning, that I'm easily influenced, but I'd prefer other explanations for why I'm still brooding over a Frank McGuinness play that several professional critics dismissed with a gaggle of tepid to savage reviews.

I saw *There Came a Gypsy Riding* at London's Almeida Theatre on January 12, 2007, the second night that it was performed, before reviews had been published, and I thought it fine and deep. I was shaken while witnessing scenes of the ultimate grief—living after the death of one's child—and I periodically burrowed into my own still self to meditate on how alone we are for the great sorrows. *With the birth of each of my children had come a new reason to silently, persistently seek favors, offer deals—as if someone were listening: Spare each of them from suffering and I'll do anything.* But McGuinness also made me laugh with his characterization of crusty old Cousin Bridget who speaks her plain truth, effectively saying to hell with tact, and my reaction came in part because Bridget is not unlike Lottie, my eighty-seven-year-old mother. When I rose from my second row seat after several rounds of robust applause, I felt smug at having discovered this jewel of a play on my own, confident that the critical ovations to come would confirm my cleverness.

While leaving the theater, my husband and I (we had been unable to sit together because only singles remained when I ordered tickets weeks before) talked about the play in tones of quiet admiration, and he mentioned that the man sitting next to him had spotted McGuinness in the audience. We began to scan the crowd as we filed into the lobby, and there he was, as pictured in the program, with a thicket of time-faded hair and beard framing weary eyes. But his living self held a glass of red wine and talked to an intense sort of woman, the type who intimidates me with an unmistakable absence of humor and warmth.

Aware that I was moved by the play, my husband urged me to go over and speak with McGuinness, ask him to sign my program, but I muttered "I can't" while hovering at the sidelines, unwilling to leave. Growing impatient, my husband gave me an actual shove in the right direction, and I found myself face to face with the playwright. Clutching my program and doing a one-handed fumble through my purse in search of a pen, I stammered out a stream of words like a nervous schoolgirl: "I never do this, but would you sign this? Your play is wonderful; thank you for writing it for us."

Frank McGuinness smiled a slow smile and then handed me his glass, took my program and pen, and asked my name. I answered "Sandra," but the voices in my head had already begun yammering *Sandra why not Sandy why not Swinburne you sound silly you should have put on make-up you should have brushed your hair your voice has a particularly nasal twang tonight.* So by the time he asked whether I was from New York, adding that he loves that city, I was reduced to saying "yes," even though the truth is "no." The truth is that I'm from a small city in upstate New York, and before that from an even smaller town, though I love New York City as well. But that was all too much to manage in words—not because of him, but because of me. Instead, I was thinking that he was kind to try to chat me up and calm me down. Then when he held out my program and thanked me for coming, I realized that Frank McGuinness looked vulnerable. I believed I saw in his eyes the *knowing* that informs the emotional isolation of the battered characters I had so recently met on the stage. I thanked him for his play one last time and rejoined my husband to begin the long walk back to the train station. It wasn't until we were hurtling through the London underground that I looked inside the program and saw, "For Sandra Love Frank McGuinness XX."

———

In the days that followed, I found myself not infrequently thinking about the play and its cast of lonely souls. Leo and Margaret McKenna join their young adult children, Louise and Simon, at the family's vacation home on the western coast of Ireland to mark what should have been the twenty-first birthday of their youngest son, Gene. But two years earlier he had made his way there on his own, overdosed with alcohol, and then slit his wrists to die on the beach. Margaret insists that there will be a birthday dinner in his honor, and "I want no weeping this weekend. That goes for all of us."

Cousin Bridget, a solitary crone living within sight of the house, discovered Gene's body (as he surely knew she would), and she still sees his wrists laid open, "Red as a robin, a June robin." She struggled hopelessly to put life back into him, and she, not his mother, was the last to hold him. Now, as Bridget approaches the McKenna door pushing an empty baby buggy found discarded on the beach that is forever Gene's, she sings an old folk song about a gypsy who comes to take children away. She playfully demonstrates for Louise that the buggy's frame steadies her walking: "Do you see the speed of me?" But she's haunted by the boy who died so young, himself a sort of gypsy riding through their lives. Turning quickly somber, she admits to being forgetful, being all-out crazy. She says she's not been the same since that day on the shore—"Jesus, the red on the white strand"—that day when Gene chose her.

Margaret, a formidable matriarch who escaped Donegal poverty by demanding perfection of herself, expects it of others as well: She refuses to tolerate fools, and on this weekend, most especially Bridget. Nobody works harder than Margaret, and years ago when her children were small she proved her determination to succeed when she lied in order to win a university position as lecturer of English literature. Leo, her seemingly genial husband, owns a pub empire that keeps him busy and makes him rich. Thinking of Gene's death, Leo explains: "We keep working. That's our way of coping. Might not be the best way, but so far—so far it's got us through."

Louise and Simon have each entered careers that disappoint Margaret, and they know it. During a talk over meal preparations, Margaret tells Simon, "We educated you and we could well have afforded you do doctorates, but you finish your master's and go to work in a bookshop. Louise does her degree and wants to teach primary school. That's what you want to do. Do it." This blunt assessment is fueled by regret that neither Louise nor Simon has her fire and drive, but she allows that they probably don't need to scrabble and claw since they'll inherit the pub fortune one day.

———

After a week of off-and-on sparring with the intricacies of human nature raised by these characters—especially the ways in which women try to manage their emotions—I decided to look for a copy of the play. When a staff member at the National Theatre shop said it was being released the following day, I again felt pleased with myself; owning the text would complete my Frank McGuinness theater experience. I would pore over the lines and parse out meaning *precisely*, differently than I could while hearing them spoken in performance. I wanted to join the coming chorus of praise for Frank McGuinness and imagined writing something about Margaret and Bridget.

Flying homeward over the Atlantic in an airplane that had been delayed due to engine trouble, I tried to distract myself with newspapers I'd stuck into my bag. I was blindsided by London theater critic Charles Spencer's column in *The Daily Telegraph*. He trashed *There Came a Gypsy Riding* with glib sound bites that buzz across the page, surely aware that their next venue is cyberspace: "The dialogue seems laborious, the characters fail to spring to detailed individual life, and there are long stretches in which McGuinness, as if painfully aware that his own writing is refusing to resonate, starts quoting bleeding chunks of Keats instead." Then, as if trying to outdo his own wit, Spencer adds: "Has anyone ever snuffed it through sheer embarrassment in a theatre?" Alternating between furious and confused, I got defensive—for Frank and for myself. Spencer's verbal strutting contributes nothing toward opening McGuinness' work for others, nothing toward quickening the viewer's or reader's own search for meaning in art. And besides, how could Spencer's response be so different from my own? *Am I easy? Sentimental?*

When I finally got home, I went online hoping to find battalions rallied in support of the play I loved. Instead I found mostly negative blurbs written by various London critics and collected by the staff of *Theatre.com*. Matt Wolf of *Theatre.com* starts off by referring to *There Came a Gypsy Riding* as "the lamentable new Frank McGuinness drama that comes across as some Irish reductio ad absurdum of many of the Greek and French neo-classical tragedies. . . ." Nicholas de Jongh of *The Evening Standard* asserts that this "unenlightening play about suicide and bereavement is couched in a defunct theatrical form and lacks a dramatic pulse. . . ." Quentin Letts of *The Daily Mail* admires Eileen Atkins' performance as Bridget, offers conditional praise for Imelda Staunton's work as Margaret (reckoning that she "did not quite crack it" in the madness scene), and suggests the script "could maybe do with one last polish." Benedict Nightingale of *The London Times* zooms in on the play's concern with suicide, then steps up to recognize it as a "dense, and, at times, a difficult play that raises plenty of pertinent and not-so-pertinent questions." Michael Billington of *The Guardian* targets the central theme of the play as "the way ancient superstitions persist even in modern materialist Ireland, and the way culture itself is death-haunted." As for craft, Billington finds that McGuinness "overstates his case" but allows that the play "offers us a fascinating portrait of the damaged Irish psyche."

What about McGuinness' study of the iron-clad pride felt by two aging women who attempt to control the pain in their lives by controlling their emotions? What about the ways in which these characters show how adept we are at hiding behind work and fate and madness to avoid confrontations with personal shortcomings? I began to wonder if my own damaged psyche might add a different dimension to the existing critical dialogue; after all, not one of the posted reviews I found was written by a woman, and it seems to me that McGuinness relies on his older female characters to do much of the story's heavy lifting. Margaret and Bridget—so different in their life choices, but so alike in their loneliness—reveal the ways we contribute to our own isolation as we struggle to conceal and protect our broken selves. More surely than the wages of suicide or the effects of Old World superstitions, a habit of loneliness defines the pain of those who remain in this gypsy's wake.

———

I entered the McKennas' lives carrying my own baggage. Margaret is the sort of woman I've watched and hated for her apparent ability to simultaneously raise a family and have a career. Like Margaret, I grabbed at education to bargain my way out of small-town ignorance, and I was the first in my family to earn a university degree. Unlike her, I found that I wanted children more than a career, and I couldn't imagine my way through the calculations of having both. All sorts of things could go wrong for children, and I couldn't risk not being on the spot and ready to intervene. I also loved being with them to share the unanticipated wonders of their childhoods. So, I waited to be needed, knowing that if I were to fail at mothering I could never forgive myself. But the price for being ever on call for a family was a sense of lacking personal accomplishment: Much of what I did on any given day—laundry, cooking, mopping, vacuuming—was undone by bedtime.

In the mornings, I hovered over breakfasts and then stood at the counter in my pajamas to pack school lunch bags. Looking across the driveway, but pretending that I wasn't, I admired my neighbor's ever-changing wardrobe as she hurried to her car, settled herself behind the steering wheel, and drove away before the buses came. Sometimes I wondered whether her children were proud of her, but in my bitter heart I hoped they resented the time she spent delivering babies at the hospital while they were stuck in after-school care. I made a show of having elaborate dinners waiting to go into the oven each evening, and I talked about cooking plans with her husband, who prepared simple meals when he got home from work. I took occasional shots at her childcare arrangements—meaning to provoke guilt—and she scored hits to my ego with sarcasm such as, "Well here's Mrs. Swinburne grocery shopping on Saturday, just like working mothers." A predictable "eating bonbons" comment once sent me to my room in tears, but in fact, we each gave as good as we got.

So when I watched the McKennas grieve for their dead child, I saw my worst nightmare enacted. My own developing psyche had been grafted onto the ancient roots of guilt and fear through a combination of religious and cultural hocus-pocus. Education and reason cannot quiet the suspicion that actions do not go unnoticed on some divine scoreboard, that there are consequences for personal failure in this world *and* the next. I stayed home those many years hoping to pay my dues, hoping that vigilance could prevent catastrophe, hoping to earn safe passage for my children.

Margaret suffers those pangs of guilt and fear but does not openly admit to them—not until the birthday weekend when Bridget surrenders the note she had found in Gene's coat but concealed for two years. The very existence of a suicide note shatters a black box full of unresolved emotions. Margaret's torment over what Gene's last words might force her to know explodes in a justification of her professional compulsions to Simon and Louise and herself: "I paid a tough price to be a teacher. I will let nothing and nobody deny me that. When I was a young one, I made a vow to each of you. I would not stand before any of you as adults and tell you you stopped me doing what I wanted. I have kept that vow. I have kept that vow perfectly." But her bravado crumbles later in a burst of irrationality when she articulates the fear that her own ambitious greed resulted in Gene's death: "You see, I cheated. I lied to get the job. I said I have no children. And it's brought me bad luck. It's why I lost Gene. He's very angry with me."

At last, I wanted to tell Margaret and those other women like her that I'm sorry.

———

For over twenty years I've suspected that I might have prevented my friend's death—not in an actual physical, mechanical way, but by having said something that could have altered the tumbling of one thing to the next. As it was, the phone call came on a Wednesday morning in July, and I can only remember the words spoken by a young girl whose voice I recognized, not what I said: "Mrs. Swinburne, my parents wanted me to call you so you'll know. My sister was killed last night. A drunk driver hit her car head on. She was alone when it happened."

I was a thirty-seven-year-old mother of four, and my friend Mary Agnes was twenty-seven and single. She was like my little sister; she shared secrets with me at my kitchen table, things she didn't want others to know, and in the end I failed to keep them. For more than twelve years she had been one of our babysitters, and exactly a week before the crash she had insisted—her gift to me—that she would stay with the children so my husband and I could go out to celebrate my birthday. After eating dinner at a restaurant, I found myself wanting to be with the kids, so we rented a video and went home early. There, the boys protested that we'd come back too soon, and my six-year-old daughter pointed out that the girls were only part way through reading *Thumbelina*. Mary Agnes promised her that they would finish the book next time.

While I tried to explain about the accident to my children, my little girl did her best to make it not so: "But we didn't finish *Thumbelina*. We were going to finish it when she came back next time." The funeral home, the church, the cemetery—each felt like a set from a movie or a play, and I didn't belong in them. Afterwards, there was no more dyed orange hair, no more hopeless love affairs, and no more law school in the fall—because those were pieces of *her* life. Could I have urged her to make different choices that might have brought a different ending? Different advice about having adventures while you're young? Different advice about different men? *You choose, I'd said. You have to choose.* I withdrew into guilty silence and sat alone in the kitchen, alone with our secrets, sobbing into old dish towels when tissues couldn't hold my tears.

—

I feel sorry for Margaret when she admits to cowardice, confessing that she knew Gene was stealing money from her but ignored it, hoping he would not steal outside the house. Fear of having to face what he did with the money kept her quiet, so she waited and hoped that her husband or her other children would notice something wrong and have the courage to intervene. But the secrets remain unspoken until it's too late. Only after Gene's final note breaks their silence do Simon and Louise spill their knowledge that he "had the makings of an addict" with all his gambling, drinking, and drug use.

Believing that literature can help translate life for the living, Margaret periodically turns to the poetry of Keats as she calibrates the dose of grief that she can bear. Helpless to make Gene's death not so, she raises Keats' immortal bird—"You were born for death, my mortal child"—in an attempt to hide behind fate. But she cannot escape the questioning. Had fate knocked her off her high horse at Gene's expense? "Would I have been better off if I'd never read a book? Stuck to where I belong down in the dirty clay, roughing it with the rest of my breed?" Even though she has made great show of leaving the primitive bonds of blood and land, Gene's death drags her back.

Until the birthday weekend, Margaret keeps her grief enshrined in silence, having cracked only once—while she was lecturing on Keats, a man who knew "he was dying too soon, a young man." She describes her failed defenses to Simon: "When I said the words, I lost my voice. Lost it completely. Stopped speaking. The students twigged it. They knew about Gene, your brother. What they didn't know was I could see his face in every one of them." But she managed, went home pretending to have the flu, and returned to work after three days as if nothing had happened. Leo accepted her story without question, perpetuating their pattern of grieving in isolation.

———

Bridget has spent her life on the desolate land near the sea, alone but for the company of devils and ghosts while she watches and waits for what is to come. At the start of the play, she offers Louise an image of her off-kilter, solitary life: "I can be merrily walking along these roads. Mile upon mile, to and fro from my house. I look in front of me—there's my head half a mile in the distance, chatting nineteen to the dozen." Life has passed her by and she's laughing, but she claims "this sorry state of affairs" can be explained: "Either it's a miracle or I'm completely mad. God's never blessed me particularly. So I rule out the miracles. That leaves madness." She remembers finding Gene's body, remembers him as a baby, remembers finding the beach property for the McKennas who bought it for "half nothing," and remembers feeling slighted by their lack of attentiveness. Then she flees those attachments with a return to the palpable presence of the empty baby buggy, her gift from the sea: "Isn't it great the way you can depend on the sea? Who knows what it will throw up next? I believe it invented the wheel."

Because Bridget's comments ramble through dangerous emotional territory with no apparent regard for others, the McKennas variously refer to her as being "child-like," "crazy," "a bitch," and "a witch." In one instance of unfiltered storytelling, Bridget finds Louise ironing and launches into her own speculations about why Margaret hates to iron, postulating that perhaps she's "lazy" or "just slow." Unable to stop there, Bridget suggests that the real explanation might be found in an accident that occurred when Margaret was seven years old: "Imagine sitting on a hot iron, imagine being that stupid." Then before parting, Bridget offers her prediction for Gene's birthday weekend: "My God, you'll shed some tears. You shouldn't. He didn't for you. Don't mind me, I'm an old fool."

But Bridget only wears fool's clothing. In reality, she is attuned to the loneliness all around her, loneliness within a family grown distant and most acutely within herself. Isolated and increasingly eccentric, she admits to Leo that Gene is not the only departed. She sees herself as having already died, with only the formalities remaining:

> "What's in store for me? A lonely old woman, pushing anyone near her far away. Sell the house—do you know why? I don't want to let you see what's coming to me. More mad, more malignant, more danger to myself. Maybe my reason will be maimed and my mind shattered, me sitting helpless in a hospital starving, dying of thirst—no family to give a tinker's curse if I live or let go."

Refusing the syrup of sympathy, and feeling abandoned by a God who has shown little caring toward her, Bridget swears that "a hard heart" is the key to survival, and that she herself is "a bride of Satan." She's even asked him to give Gene back: "He, Satan, did not believe in resurrections. That was the other boyo's business." Still, under the antics of a madwoman Bridget cherishes the role for which she was chosen in the aberrant pieta scene on the beach: "I cradled him in my arms. I comforted him. He was like my baby. My beautiful baby. Silent—not crying—in my arms."

My widowed mother is a prickly old lady who lives alone, and like Bridget, she is full of hard observations and plenty of advice, claiming only to be "telling it like it is." When I phone to check on her, she gets right down to the business of reporting news from home. Almost without fail, the story reaches its climax with, "And I told them . . . ."

A few people jokingly refer to my mother as the village mayor. Mention anyone living in that town of about two hundred where she's spent most of her life, and she'll tell you whether they "amount to a tinker's damn," and she'll throw in that they do or don't have "a pot to piss in." Her collection of friends, already plundered by death, continues to thin as she lets loose firecracker opinions on welfare ("I don't mind helping people in trouble, but I'll be damned if I'm going to support people who sit on their asses and don't even try to get a job"), credit cards ("I told my neighbor Donnie to cut up all those credit cards; nobody needs more than one and they'll just get him in trouble. He's too stupid to have credit cards"), and suspect priests ("Father had that fella staying at the rectory to play around with").

My mother and her friend Alice used to talk on the phone early each morning, but there are plenty of reasons why Alice doesn't call her anymore. Now, like the proverbial broken record, my mother reviews Alice's drinking problem, without a shred of sympathy, whenever conversation lags: "She'll sit home and drink alone, or she'll go out looking for someone to drink with. Why one night, Janey heard Alice's garage door open at ten o'clock and her car drive away. Hey, come on now. She was probably going out to the Legion Hall to sit and drink beer. Not that it's any surprise; when her husband was alive they were always propped up at a beer joint. Listen to this: The sheriff called Jen one night and asked if she knew Alice because he had her sitting in his office. Alice had taken off in her car and gotten lost, didn't know where she was. Jen went and picked her up and took her home. One of these days her big buddies the priests are gonna get a call. I don't know why her family doesn't come up and do something about her."

My mother wants to stay in the house where she's lived for over sixty years, and she'll never admit that it's lonely. She is happy to visit me, and she talks incessantly from the moment that we're together. For a while I can listen to the same stories that I've heard once or twice or twenty times before, but eventually I make it clear that I have work to do. After a couple days she begins to miss her own house, points out that she can't just sit around with nothing to do. The problem isn't actually so much a lack of doing as it is an absence of something to watch, something other than me as I'm reading or writing at the computer, and she's soon bored. So I try to be more entertaining and plan a morning of shopping errands, or I cook something new which gets her interested in recipes and food talk.

When we drive back to the house where I grew up, she sometimes wants me to fill the two bird feeders outside the kitchen windows because she likes to watch the flurry of visitors—robins, cardinals, and goldfinches—as they come looking for sunflower seeds. If there's snow she'll let me shovel, but I can please her most if I haul out the bucket and towels to wash the four windows that wrap around her breakfast nook.

Alone day after day, she pours herself a cup of coffee and settles into her chair at the head of the table to watch the townspeople perform. She watches the workers at the town barn across the road as they load their trucks and head out to patch or plow. She watches anyone who drives up or down the street, pulls into the driveway next door, goes to mass at the church on the corner—and she can report whether there are lights on in the rectory. She gathers clues and pieces together a certain version of life occurring on the other side of the glass.

———

The McKennas dredged up my memories of another death too soon, another summer morning that was shattered with a phone call impossibly similar to the one before. This time the caller was a friend's seventeen-year-old son, who said, "Mrs. Swinburne, my brother is dead. His plane crashed." An eighteen-year-old brother and son, a pilot with three years of experience, was flying a small plane back from his grandparents' house on a Saturday morning when it crashed into Lake Ontario. Later that day, amidst remembering adolescent frustrations and flashes of anger, someone asked, "Could it have been suicide?" I said, "I don't think so," because I couldn't say, "I don't know."

I regularly claimed that my friend, the mother of those boys, was the nicest woman in upstate New York. She was a stay-at-home mom who worried incessantly over her own children and everyone else's. No matter what anyone needed, she tried to figure out a way to help; if nobody needed a driver, a babysitter, or a multi-purpose volunteer, she baked for someone, for the fun of a surprise or as therapy for whatever worries might be hovering over a particular household. Those of us lucky enough to know her sampled a fantasy assortment of new cookies that she shared in the bleachers, left on doorsteps, or sent home with children. When the father of a boy on one of the Little League teams she loved to watch struggled to gain weight after cancer treatments, he needed, and she delivered, freshly baked pies. Once when I mentioned that I had a headache, that night's dinner magically appeared. Some of her friends joked about the possibility of faking "need" to get food from her.

My friend was silenced by the plane crash; for days she sat waiting for whatever was to come next. Questions begged for answers as weeks became months: What to do with a boy's clothes and sneakers and treasures? What to do but sit in his room amidst all his things? What to do but sell the house and hope that laughing boys would once again play in that room?

I thought about the death of my friend's son after reading Charles Spencer's complaint that when the McGuinness play ends, "neither the characters, nor the audience, are any closer to understanding the dead young man or his motives." But a gypsy can come riding in search of Gene McKenna—or my friend's son—and leave without explanation. How can it be that even the most devoted love and vigilance do not stop death from stealing the young? Can we only understand the questions? *Should I have kept him from going? But he was so happy when I drove him to the airport, talking and laughing. Do you think there was something wrong with the plane? Could he have fallen asleep? What happened over the lake in the blue, blue sky of a summery morning?*

———

I suppose I'm no closer to understanding why critics dismissed *There Came a Gypsy Riding* with so little regard. But I've found that by studying lines and remembering, I hear Margaret and Bridget say things that my mother, my career-minded neighbor, my grieving friend, and I have been unable to say. I suspect that the loneliness of women binds me to McGuinness' characters, on the stage and in the text—the same loneliness that explains why my copy of Norman Maclean's *A River Runs Through It* falls open to page 102, where a mother reacts to news of her son's death:

> My mother turned and went to her bedroom where, in a house full of men and rods and rifles, she had faced most of her great problems alone. She was never to ask me a question about the man she loved most and understood least. Perhaps she knew enough to know

that for her it was enough to have loved him. He was probably the only man in the world who had held her in his arms and leaned back and laughed.

That mother's loss quite simply breaks my heart, sentimental as that may sound.

Beyond the study of grief and loneliness, Frank McGuinness wants his characters to learn something about how to live. In the rage of emotions following the surrender of Gene's suicide note, the family members divulge secrets that have festered within, and their relationships seem doomed. But each begins to see that hope is possible only through tenderness and forgiveness. When the McKennas are packed for their return to Dublin, Bridget assures Leo that she'll remain next to the sea, with Gene. Waiting with the baby buggy, she asks when she'll see them again, adding, "I miss you. It's lonely."

For Frank Love Sandra XX

Sorrows and Silence

"You got to keep a constant eye on wastage, constant.
What you've got to understand is the nature of the goods.
Which is perishable."
—Graham Swift, *Last Orders*

Too late. That's when we often discover what's what in life. In Graham Swift's novel *Last Orders*, that's when Jack and Amy Dodds tally the costs of being fifty years married without having talked about why duties keep them apart. Too late. That's also when a character in a true story, a woman named Sandy, started wishing she could make things right with the people who are missing from her life, some of them never actually there to lose, some of them dead before she understood the finality of "last orders" before closing. Sandy's story begins in lots of places, places that she can't find with a map, places that began to crowd into her head while she read about Jack and Amy.

In fiction, the telling begins when Jack's friends are gathered at their regular pub in working-class London (The Coach that doesn't go anywhere, they joke) to begin a pilgrimage to Margate where they will scatter his remains into the sea from the pier—the very end of the pier. That's what Jack wanted. But Amy is missing from the turnout because it's Thursday, and her absence combines with Jack's presence in the ash-filled jar to set everyone adrift through the remembered past.

Sandra Swinburne

JACK AND AMY

Jack Dodds and eighteen-year-old Amy Mitchell meet during the heat of summer at Wick's Farm in Kent where they work as transient hop pickers. One night they take a walk that ends in a hop-bin, "like two rabbits in a sack," and conceive a child that becomes their reason to marry. Then, on June 1, 1939, they find themselves the parents of a "dud" baby. Doctors can't do anything to fix little June with her abnormal head on a normal body, and she is sent to a "home for the hopeless." For Jack, once was enough; he refuses to go with Amy to see June, and does not ask about her. As the years pass, he's satisfied that his duties are fulfilled by having married Amy, served courageously in the army during World War II, and accepted his place in the family butcher business—which meant forfeiting his dream of becoming a doctor. None of this is to say that he doesn't care for Amy in his own way; it's just that Amy, by refusing to forget about June, chooses her over him.

Amy holds onto Jack even though when June arrives she "felt him tug away, tug and twist and turn against me at the same time, as if it really was all my fault now, my problem, not his." Feeling desperate at eighteen, she finagles the money for a belated seaside honeymoon at Margate where she dresses in her new outfit, "undies," and swimsuit ("what hard-nosed little tricksies we can be") in an attempt to be the woman of Jack's dreams. On the boardwalk, Jack shoots tin ducks and wins a prize for Amy; she chooses a stuffed teddy bear—excitedly hugging it rather than Jack. Then as she bends to fix her shoe at the end of the Jetty, he throws the child's toy into the sea. Amy should get the message, but she's unwilling to give up. While Jack is away during the war, she scoops up little Vince Pritchett, a normal baby whose parents were killed in a bomb raid.

Jack and Amy stay together through a lifetime, in spite of some infidelity (he with prostitutes, she with his friend Ray), and in spite of a threatening emotional sea that each fails to navigate. Because she believes that mothers must *mother*, Amy continues to make her usual bus trips each Monday and Thursday to see the daughter who "hasn't even got the brains of a child of two." On June's fiftieth birthday, Amy tries to get Jack to join her for a celebration visit, and he suggests that perhaps he'll close the shop early and meet her there. But when the time comes, he explains to a friend that he can't make himself go: "'I knew I couldn't do it, I couldn't change, not like that.'" The friend, an undertaker who once called on Jack to help prepare a corpse, knows for a fact that "Jack Dodds was only ever squeamish about going to see his daughter. His own flesh and blood."

Jack figures to distract Amy from his failure to visit June by announcing that his all-work-and-no-play approach to life is finished. After years of cutting chops and grinding chuck for the local housewives, he is finally forced to admit that he can't turn a profit anymore. He must sell the business to pay off his debts, but the version he tells Amy is that he'll retire and they'll become "'new people'" in a little retirement cottage in Margate. She knows life's not so forgiving: "As if we could put the clock back and start off again where it all stopped. Second honeymoon. As if Margate was another word for magic." When she mentions June, he replies, "'If I can give up being Jack Dodds, family butcher, then you can give up going on that fool's errand every week.'" But before Jack can press ahead with his plan, he is diagnosed with stomach cancer. And even as he's dying, Jack and Amy find that they still cannot put words on certain things they've felt through the years.

VINCE

Until Vince is around ten, he does not know about June and does not know that he's adopted; when kids at school tease him, "*Vincey's got a sister, face like a blister,*" he fights them.

Jack won't talk about the daughter who isn't right, or about how she's the reason he has a son who isn't really his. But Amy finally insists that he explain to Vince where babies come from, two babies in particular. One Sunday, when the three of them are loaded into the meat van for a drive to the seashore at Margate, Jack turns off and goes to Wick's Farm where he and Amy met. Parked on a hilltop, Amy announces, "'They call Kent the Garden of England,'" then signals Jack with a nod that he needs to take Vince for a walk through the fields. Jack's nervous muddling of the facts causes Vince to feel so frightened and confused that he interprets the day's lesson to be that babies come from hops. "It wasn't Jack and Amy who picked my hops, they picked someone else's hops. She was called June. So it was true what the other kids said, the ones I hit. *Vincey's got a sister.* But it wasn't true as well, because my hops were picked by someone else, they were picked by—"

Vince's childhood also bears the mark of Amy's addition to the story, that Jack never wanted to tell him anything about June and his birth parents—"[t]hough how he thought he could keep me fooled beats me." Amy explains "that June was an accident, an accident of birth," in that she and Jack did not want to have her, leading him to understand he was *chosen*. Vince knows that what Amy really wants is a normal daughter, like his friend Sally who used to go to Margate with them on Sundays, and what Jack really wants is a son who will take over Dodds and Son. Hoping to diminish Jack's power, and feeling tricked about both the past and the present, Vince musters boyish determination to confront Amy and volunteer for what Jack refuses to do: "'Take me to see her, take me to see June.'"

As soon as he's old enough, Vince signs on for five years in the armed service to escape Jack's expectations. There he develops a plan that will keep him from being forced into the meat business when he gets out: He learns about car engines so he can dream his own "Dodds Motors" into existence. According to Vince, a motor can be understood, taken apart and put back together; a classy car provides a man with the best sort of relationship: "It's a mate. It won't ask no questions, it won't tell no lies. It's somewhere you can be and be who you are."

The Last Good Obsession

TO MARGATE

When the time comes for Jack's final wish to be fulfilled, Vince arrives at The Coach in a royal blue Mercedes to pick up Jack's three best friends and the jar of ashes. But grudges and secrets compound to create an unruly elephant in the car: Ray loves Amy and they had a brief affair, Lenny has fantasized about Amy for years ("undressing her in my heart"), Vince left Lenny's daughter Sally carrying "one little unborn sod" when he packed off for military duty, and Vic once caught a glimpse of Amy and Ray together, but never told Jack.

Emotions spill over as each man makes his private journey with Jack. During the day-long procession that includes lunch with plenty of drinks, respects paid at a war memorial, and a tour of Canterbury Cathedral, the real adventures unfold in dark interiors where troubled minds confront personal failures. Vince detours to Wick's Farm where he "splutters like he's trying to announce something" while scattering a bit of Jack's ashes in the field: "'This is where,' he says wiping his face. 'This is where.'" On reaching Margate, they find "the sea's grey and thick and churny like the sky," like their own thoughts. Under the gathering storm, they walk Jack's ashes to the very end of the pier where a piece of the old Jetty that washed away years ago is still visible. Each man scoops a handful of ash and "the Jack who once walked around, is carried away by the wind, is whirled away by the wind till the ash becomes wind and the wind becomes Jack what we're made of."

AMY

She remembers the end, when Jack seemed to know that their life could have been different, but he cannot say the words, only "looks at me like he's sorry for having left it too late, for having to be going just when he was going to put things right." Amy knows that Jack Dodds was never going to change, and that he didn't even look that sorry.

But memories of a different Jack can well up, and there she is back on a hillside at Wick's Farm to hear him say, "'You're beautiful, d'you know that? You're beautiful.'" She remembers Margate—the Jetty, the beach, and the rides at the amusement park called Dreamland. She sees "the big hunk of man" she'd kept wanting in spite of all his stubbornness and failures, and knows that she'll "always see Jack's face, like a little photo inside my head." With Jack's ashes en route to Margate, the bus carries Amy to June, to say goodbye. She tells herself: "I've got to be my own woman now."

JIM AND EVELYN

Another telling can begin amidst lived lives, in December of 1939 when Evelyn gave birth to a son with Down syndrome, a chromosome mix-up at number twenty-one that causes varying degrees of developmental disability. But the doctor did not tell her that he suspected this abnormality, even though there are characteristic physical signs—a single crease across palms, small folds at the inner edge of eyelids, and poor muscle tone—that point to the diagnosis. Evelyn and her husband Jim thought they were taking home a normal baby.

By standards of the day, Evelyn was not considered a young mother. She had married late, having already turned thirty-two, and surely had considered again and again the possibility that she would remain a single woman who worked as a bank teller and lived with her widowed mother in Montreal. Family members must have felt anxious when they arranged for her to meet the unmarried son of former neighbors, a shy engineer whose parents had emigrated from England. She must have felt transported onto the pages of a romance novel when she found both love and marriage with Jim.

In the 1937 portrait of their wedding party, Evelyn stands next to her unsmiling new husband with their shoulders just barely touching. She looks straight into the camera all clear-eyed and guileless. She wears a long-sleeved, shirt-waist gown, and the only hint of daring comes from the tilt of her hat, a close-fitted cap with a pouf of short veil that shimmers behind her neck. Because she otherwise exemplifies dignified simplicity, it seems probable that the hat was positioned by Dottie, her youngest sister and maid of honor, the little beauty at Evelyn's left who flirts with the photographer or the camera itself. The secret dreams that flicker behind this bouquet of still faces have long since evanesced as dust returned to dust. This photo and the bridal lingerie, the ivory silk charmeuse tap pants and camisole that lay carefully folded in an old mahogany dresser forty-seven years later, are the last vestiges of that day.

After the wedding, the newly married couple settled in Syracuse, New York where Jim drove the easy commute to the Carrier Corporation each workday, and Evelyn, who didn't know how to drive, busied herself with the chores delegated to housewives. They eventually bought a house on Charmouth Drive, a tree-lined street in a quiet neighborhood where they could comfortably raise their family. It seemed like a place where they could live out their married lives, and in fact they did, but not for the number of years that they had hoped. Jim died suddenly in 1962 from an aortic aneurysm, leaving behind Evelyn and three sons: twenty-three-year-old Peter, who lived in a state institution for the mentally disabled; nineteen-year-old Andrew, who was a sophomore at Brown; and Paul, twelve years old and living at home. More accurately, Jim left that family to the care of his middle son, who understood that his shattered mother and little lost brother needed him. Happy times in Providence were over.

Evelyn's family feared that Jim's death would be her final undoing. She had struggled with depression for years. There were periods of calm, but there were also waves of tormenting thoughts that battered at her defenses until the mother could not function as the mother. After Jim's funeral, her sisters from Canada and her sister-in-law from England's Lake District took turns visiting, hoping to stabilize a world unmoored by illness and grief. There were appointments with doctors and hospital stays; there was also a twelve-year-old boy to be looked after. The aunts gave a week here and there, but each had a family of her own. Reality dictated that long-term responsibility rested with Andrew.

A SON'S TO-DO LIST

1. Transfer to Syracuse University, live at home, switch majors (psychology requirements easier to fulfill than science)
2. Attend classes, read texts, write papers
3. Get groceries, with or without Mother
4. Drive Mother to doctor appointments
5. Take Mother to visit Peter when she asks
6. Attend parents' nights at Paul's school
7. Make sure Paul has friends over
8. Apply to medical school
9. Accept offer from Upstate Medical School
10. Study harder, work longer
11. Take Paul to visit colleges and help with his applications
12. Move Paul off to college where he'll become an engineer—like Dad
13. With Mother stable, move into own apartment near hospitals
14. Drift into Johnny Lamp's for a few beers

SANDY

As fall semester 1971 got underway at SU, she sometimes wondered how it happened that she was a senior nursing student. She'd gotten through the first three years with good grades, but was never quite sure that she actually wanted to be a nurse. After all, a flip of the coin had determined her choice; even the brightest girls in the rural community where she grew up didn't imagine further than nurse, teacher, nurse, teacher, one or the other. She wondered whether she might be better suited to life on the other side of the coin.

Never mind that she fainted from hangover complications one morning in the operating room just as the orthopedic surgeon began sawing on a leg. There were other times when she felt as if she had a small, rewarding role in an episode of the *Dr. Kildare* television series that she'd watched during high school. The doctors and nurses could be inspiring (not to mention fun), and the patient success stories kept everyone going. But her tolerance of hospitals had been tested the previous summer when she worked forty hours a week on a general medical floor called First Lipe, where many of the patients were elderly and some were demented. She had dreaded pulling duty among the withered blooms in the women's ward referred to as the Rose Garden, and she'd spent what seemed like more than her share of time tending their dentures, soiled sheets, and lost minds. She preferred pediatrics; in fact, she loved working with children. The only drawback there was the need to steel her emotions so that she could face the sad stories and hopeless cases without crying all the time.

The reward for those long days and nights rotating between all three shifts on First Lipe was money enough to make payments on a Triumph Spitfire convertible. As if looking at the sleek red car wasn't excitement enough, climbing into the black leather seat and gripping the gear shift was better than just about anything. When she cruised with the top down and the radio playing, she became someone else, someone adventurous. Her clutch control on steep campus hills improved quickly—less revving and stalling. No more begging for rides or being talked into hitchhiking. With classes looking manageable, her possessions settled into slum housing at the edge of campus, and the fall dating game catching fire, she thought life just might be on the upswing.

One September Saturday night, she faced the mirror of discontent and tried to get the clothes, make-up, and hair just right before driving downtown to Johnny Lamp's, a favorite after-hours stop for doctors and nurses. Premeditated effort meant she was slender and tanned with her streaked blonde hair pinned in a chignon, and she was ready to test her theory that a snug-fitting sweater with a midi-length, belted skirt and high heels produced an aloof look, an icy challenge. Even though she had just turned twenty-one, she was making up for lost time after having ended a yearlong engagement that had seemed much longer; the time was right to look for fun in wrong places, places like Lamp's.

Smoking a Newport and gripping a Budweiser, she traded news with a few nurses and medical students until she spotted a doctor she recognized from First Lipe—tall, serious, good-looking, and known through the grapevine to be single. She repositioned herself so that she could small-talk him about the hospital ward they had in common, and she soon learned that his name was Andrew. He was finishing his medical residency and, funny, they shared a shameless penchant for fast, foreign cars, his being a red Datsun 240Z. After a couple hours of comparing Jaguar fantasies and stories from the Rose Garden, he asked her to go out with him the next Saturday. He suggested that they drive out of town and go to a restaurant on a secluded lake. She began to plan what she'd wear, what was nice enough.

EVELYN

Evelyn was a widow of nine years and living alone on Charmouth Drive when Andrew brought a young woman named Sandy over for dinner on a week night in late October. The three of them sat in the dining room and made cautious conversation around a linen-covered table set with Waterford crystal, English silver, and plates decorated with a pattern called Desert Rose. Evelyn couldn't hide how pleased she was that her son had brought someone to meet her, someone he described as "special." She had cooked a roast as if for Sunday dinner, and made butterscotch pie for dessert because it had always been the boys' favorite. She wanted everything to be right. There she was, being the mother, sitting at the head of the table, trying not to seem anxious while talking with her son and his girlfriend.

ANDREW AND SANDY

Time spooled on fast forward and they spent every available moment together; within two months, she had moved some of her things into his apartment to simplify getting to work and school in the morning. When he returned from the hospital, they shared food she had prepared, and they clung to each other in an extra-long single bed. He told her about Peter, his older brother whom he only knew through occasional visits to the institution where he lived. He told her about "never having been so smart as when he was nineteen," but then, hit with his father's death, realizing too late how little he actually knew. And he told her about his mother's illness, about how it had taught him to simply do what needs to be done without dwelling on what should be or could be.

There was something she'd never told anyone, but she told him: She had a half-sister she'd never seen except in photographs. When Sandy was five or six years old, she'd noticed a picture of a little girl on a bureau at her grandmother's house, and each time she'd seen it, she felt hurt and wondered who it was. Why would her father's mother keep that big picture of a stranger right in the front room? Why had her grandmother chosen another little girl over her? She never asked anything about the girl, not even her name; jealousy kept her silent. Besides, that grandmother lived two hours away and Sandy didn't go there very often; her sister Karen, who was three years older, made overnight visits now and then, but Sandy got homesick and wanted to stay in her own house. That grandmother scared her just a bit.

When Sandy was around seven, she and Karen returned from school to find their mother crying; not the loud sobbing kind of crying, just the snuffly kind. "I need to talk to you girls," was how her mother started, and then came the news: "Your dad was married once before and he has a daughter named Judy who lives with her mother. Your grandmother is upset that we haven't told you, and Uncle Allen wrote a letter threatening to tell you if we didn't. Your dad is afraid you won't love him anymore, so make sure you tell him that you do." That was all. Sandy and her sister said okay and went upstairs to the room they shared, but did not talk about Judy or the other wife—a silence that, even as she told the story to Andrew, seemed unbelievable.

When Sandy's father returned from work later in the day, he went to the living room and turned on the television; she and her sister were idling in the kitchen near their mother who nudged them to go say what they were supposed to say. They took turns, each hugging their father and saying "I love you," but he didn't say anything, just returned their hugs. Neither her mother nor her father said anything more about Judy, ever again, and after that grandmother died, the photograph disappeared.

By late November, all the secrets had been told. Sandy and Andrew decided to have a small wedding between semesters. He surprised her with tickets to Aruba for their honeymoon, and she began to shop for a dress. They drove to her parents' house to tell them the news, and it was welcomed with a vague sense of pride and relief; her father told her to choose a restaurant for a reception and the bill would be taken care of. When Andrew told his friends that they were getting married, one said: "Are you crazy? That's never going to last!" Andrew and Sandy laughed, knowing that it would. For Christmas, they drove to Montreal to join his mother and younger brother at Aunt Dot's, then made the rounds among the other Canadian relatives to spread the word about their January wedding. The old aunts looked delighted to see the young couple; they desperately wanted Andrew to have the happiness they believed he deserved.

EVELYN

Back at Charmouth Drive, Evelyn wanted to explain to Sandy about Peter. Slipping back through the years to when she was a new mother, she described how Peter had seemed slower to do things than other babies, and that she and Jim had been concerned: "Around the time that Peter turned two and should have been getting into mischief, he wasn't; something wasn't right. Our family doctor finally told us, when Peter was three, that his failure to develop was caused by Down syndrome. We had no idea he had trouble like that. Then the doctor recommended that we put him in a special hospital where he could be cared for properly. He told us that we couldn't take care of him at home, and he said there was a private hospital in the Adirondacks where he would get the care he needed."

As if convincing herself all over again, Evelyn stressed the doctor's authority amidst the helplessness that she had felt: "It was nice there; they knew how to help Petey. But that hospital closed down after a few years and he was moved to the State Hospital at Rome. The doctor said we couldn't take care of him at home." Taking out a family photo album, she pointed to a black and white snapshot of a little blonde boy, eyes like almonds, sitting on a wooden scooter. He looked startlingly like photographs of Andrew as a child, except not right.

SANDY

Babies. She wanted to take care of babies, so as soon as she graduated in June, she applied and was hired for a staff nurse position in a neonatal intensive care unit. She was terrified by the assortment of miniature parts: Their arms were like limp little carrots, each toe no more than a niblet, and here and there a head swollen with too much fluid. She was terrified of so many fine-gauge needles with their plastic butterfly wings stilled by tape on transparent skin. And the lengths of soft plastic tubes disappearing down tiny nostrils, and respirators pumping air into unready lungs. But she would learn what they needed, and when they were well enough she would wrap them in soft cotton blankets and hold them.

When David was brought to the nursery, she knew he would be hers. Each of the nurses had favorites, and once the head nurse knew who was attached to which baby, those affections were respected in the care assignments. Why not allow for the healing powers of love and touch? So for nearly three months at forty hours per week, she tended David, a little boy with Down syndrome who had been born too soon. Respirator, IV, blood samples, heart, lungs, skin, alertness, diapers. She smoothed his shock of silky black hair, caressed his cheek with one finger, and did her best to comfort his devoted parents who had been surprised by a late-in-life pregnancy.

ROCHESTER

That's where Sandy's real life began. One month after they moved to Rochester, New York, she gave birth to her own baby boy whom a visitor described as "a cute little bald pip." Love and responsibility overwhelmed her; each rash and fussy spell was cause for worry lest she miss a symptom of something serious. Was he hungry? Was she producing enough breast milk? Was he crying and refusing to nurse because she had eaten garlic or because he was ill? But such a darling baby! When he was three months old, she dressed him in a blue and white sweater outfit and took him to a department store photographer, convinced that he would win first prize in the most beautiful baby contest.

A second and a third child arrived, each perfectly beautiful. Yet the duties of motherhood seemed to require more hours than each day allowed. As the children got older, demands seemed to increase: If the eight-year-old fell from his bike, the four-year-old needed help in the bathroom, and the two-year-old chose right then to begin screaming in her bed. Some days seemed inordinately long.

The Last Good Obsession

EVELYN

Part of Evelyn's last night on Charmouth Drive passed at a raised window in a second-floor bedroom. The next morning, she was found broken but alive in the rose garden below. Her neighbor phoned the son who was a doctor in Rochester to tell him that an ambulance had taken his seventy-eight-year-old mother to Upstate Medical Center.

Andrew arrived at the hospital to find that his mother's bones needed pinning and her mind once again needed mending, but against all probability she would survive. Evelyn was confused about what had happened, as if the fall were some inexplicable accident. Surgery followed by psychiatric consultation marked the start of a journey that led to first one nursing home and then another. During those early months of recovery, Andrew snapped a photograph of Evelyn holding his fourth child, the first meeting of grandmother and grandchild. Looking soothed with the bundle in her arms, she smiles for the camera, from a distance.

Evelyn's physical and mental condition improved over time, and she was eventually able to walk with a walker and enjoy the company of some semi-lucid inhabitants at her last place of residence, a nursing home three miles from Andrew and his family. Her son Paul with his wife and young son occasionally visited from Oswego, the site of a nuclear power plant where Paul worked as an engineer. Evelyn loved seeing them, seeing evidence that her youngest boy had grown into a happy man. But a room in a nursing home isn't a home. While she was sleeping, someone pried the diamond out of the engagement ring Jim had given her. Her clothes disappeared from the closet or never returned from the laundry. The food tasted terrible. And the long days and nights were lonely. Photographs of Jim, her two youngest sons, and her smiling grandchildren decorated the room where she lived to be ninety-one years old.

SANDY

She made herself walk through the front doors of nursing homes, and made herself negotiate the gauntlet of sunken faces with hollow eyes staring out from behind big bifocals, perhaps even trifocals. A pungent brew of talcum powder and dribbled urine. The Rose Garden had smelled like that; all the nursing homes smelled like that. When she took some of the children with her, she watched that they didn't trip someone wielding a walker or get in the way of a wheelchair. *Smile say Hi how are you today Sure is cold outside but nice and warm in here Gosh that's a pretty lap blanket you have That's a nice tote bag attached to your walker How was lunch Smile til your face hurts*

At first, she tried to do something useful for Evelyn, like clip and clean neglected fingernails. She took nail polish remover with her since some of the nursing assistants seemed to pass through the rooms painting old ladies' fingernails with iridescent pink lacquer that soon turned grotesque. Better when she had something she could do while she was there rather than just sit trying to think of chit-chat. And she didn't mind shopping for underwear or robes to replace those that were worn or had disappeared; she could do that.

The visits felt like torture; she preferred that Evelyn be brought over to the house for a meal and time with the children. But then that began to feel uncomfortable as well. There was nothing left to say that could be said, because the truth was that she blamed her mother-in-law for not having been the *mother* when her sons needed her. She stopped going to visit and felt anxious and depressed and guilty. She told herself that she would go, but she didn't. And then, it was too late. Her mother-in-law was dust in a box.

OAKWOOD

After the winter ground had thawed, a service for Evelyn was scheduled at Oakwood Cemetery in Syracuse. Andrew and Sandy's oldest son, a junior in college, was studying in Australia and they had decided not to tell him about his grandmother's death until he returned. The three younger children, each dressed as if for church, piled into the back seats of a dark blue and gray Suburban while their parents buckled into the front seats. They headed due east along the course of the Erie Canal, past Montezuma Swamp with its wildlife sanctuary, past the Carrier Dome at SU, and through the cemetery gates to a grassy plot where Evelyn's ashes were buried next to Jim's.

READING

Sandy's first reading of Graham Swift's *Last Orders* took place in 1999 when she found it in a book swap bag. She had seen the title on her list of Booker Prize winners, so she anticipated a good read and was not disappointed. But she did not recognize herself in Amy or Jack or Vince; that would come later. During a son's visit home from college, she handed him the text with its shades-of-gray cover and said, "Read this; you'll like it." A book on the floor next to a bed, a tall glass of water . . . too late to say, "Move the glass," and even after being carefully dried, the pages remained buckled and stained.

In 2002, *Last Orders* unexpectedly resurfaced in her reading life when, having fallen for Faulkner during a literature class, she immersed herself in his Yoknapatawpha version of life. Hearing an Englishman at a Faulkner conference comment that Graham Swift had written a book inspired by *As I Lay Dying*, she remembered *Last Orders* and read it again, more carefully, to ponder similarities. Like Addie Bundren, Jack Dodds wields immense power, even after death, as those who journey toward the fulfillment of his final wishes struggle with the burdens of choice and memory.

That second reading was all about writing and influence. Swift borrows Faulkner's form, builds his story through the accumulation of alternating individual narratives titled with each speaker's name. Addie's youngest son Vardaman's complete chapter, "My mother is a fish," morphs into one of Vince's chapters that reads, "Old buggers." There are other humorous comparisons as well: Anse Bundren finds a new wife, "a kind of duck-shaped woman" who owns "one of them little graphophones," while Amy Dodds considers the role "*little* man" Ray and his deluxe camper van will play in her future after she satisfies her duty to tell June the truth.

Then, after five years, Sandy began to think about *Last Orders* again, for what it says about mothering, and she read it for a third time. But that reading was different; that reading caused her to know and remember. She saw some of herself in Amy—"a mother was a mother." Yet Swift's portrayal of Amy is not meant to be all Madonna, and Sandy recognized herself in a few of the less admirable characteristics as well.

There are many ways of being "hard-nosed little tricksies." Amy knows and uses the time-tested feminine tradition of acquiring power through martyrdom and sex. For starters, Amy is pretty, and then she designs an identity out of sacrifice, turning herself into "brave little Amy." Admired by men for her looks and her never-a-whimper-devotion to June, she subtly diminishes other wives and her own husband in a stealthy bid to elicit sympathy from a select, masculine audience. There is no mention of female friends in Amy's life; her consuming focus is to bear up and carry on with her duties, her duties to June.

Amy also knows how to stubbornly hold a conviction, without budging, throughout a lifetime. As if having decided when you're right you're right, she nurses a grudge far better than she knows how to negotiate the moves toward forgiveness. Passing silent judgment against Jack, she saves her bitter thoughts for the interior monologues that race through her head. Even as she rides the bus to visit June while Jack's ashes are en route to Margate, she's still festering: "That your own daddy who never came to see you, who you never knew because he never wanted to know you, that your own daddy." Fifty years is a long time to nurse anger without finding a way to let go, yet, as evidenced by Amy's life, a feat that can be managed.

Then there was Jack to consider. Sandy saw that, like him, she had failed to fulfill family duties that were basic and human. Like him, just when she thought she might do the right thing, the time came and she couldn't take the necessary steps to offer comfort. Like him, she fixated on certain duties, neglected others, and then it was too late.

And Vince—*"Vincey's got a sister."*

POST MORTEM

Peter died a middle-aged man in his forties at the state hospital where he had lived most of his life. David, that other baby with almond-shaped eyes, lived at home with his parents for several months, then died from pneumonia complications before reaching those toddler years when other children get into mischief.

When Sandy was thirty-three, her father died from stroke complications without ever having talked to her about the little girl in the photograph. At eighty-seven, her mother has not spoken a word about Judy since that one day of disclosure.

But the revenant hovers in the corners of unfinished stories. Not long ago, a photograph of Judy taken at age four or five made the journey from a great-great aunt's desk, to a second cousin, who gave it to another cousin, who gave it to Sandy saying, "I thought you might like to have this; it's a picture of your half-sister Judy." Sandy could see that, except for a more pointed hairline, the little face looks startlingly like her own childhood photographs.

If Judy were still alive, she would be around sixty-six years old. Sandy wondered if there are adult children somewhere near or far, half-cousins to her own children. One day she took the photograph from inside the cluttered dresser drawer where she keeps it, and she looked at the fine hair that's carefully parted and clipped in a barrette, but on the side opposite her own part. The eyes seemed sad. She tried to imagine that little girl's life. Then she began to wonder whether she might find the grown-up woman, Judy, her half-sister. There had been other times when she'd imagined their meeting, imagined the two of them talking and liking each other, but she'd always put those thoughts aside. She couldn't ask her mother about Judy; dredging up unhappy memories might upset her. *Or would finally talking about the secret be a relief for both mother and daughter?* The internet might provide clues. Or she might ask her father's last living cousins? She would have to think, have to decide before it's too late. Because, in fact, we are all perishable goods.

Vanishing Woman Seeks Adventure

As things developed, she was to have
all manner of revelations.
—Thomas Pynchon, *The Crying of Lot 49*

Picture this: A suburban housewife in her late thirties drives a behemoth blue Chevy Suburban to her children's suburban school to deliver the forgotten lunch sack containing an assortment of healthy foods, each carefully wrapped and layered, that she had recently gripped in her hand while jogging in futile pursuit of an unwavering school bus with its backseat riders smiling and waving at her panting in a faded "he got the trip she got the Harvard sweatshirt," red velour shorts, and sneakers as they all made way down the tree-lined street—past the trim working mothers in their linen suits carrying leather briefcases out to their sleek taupe sedans that would soon glide into parking garages next to glassy-high downtown professional buildings and past the yard crews already raking and mowing the two-career family lawns. Then she finds herself flustered upon meeting one of her children's teachers in the side hall of the school, flustered when she realizes how she must look, flustered when the teacher asks, "How are you?" and flustered when she hears her own voice say, "We're fine."

Sandra Swinburne

What Follows Once upon a Time?

As I settled into my first reading of *The Crying of Lot 49*, I practically begged Tom Pynchon for a wild ride into mystery and paranoia. I wanted escape from the familiar; I wanted to feel drunk on intrigue. *Hit the gas, spin out on the turns, lose control.* Road tripping with protagonist Oedipa Maas took me out of suburbia, onto the freeway, and "into San Narciso on Sunday, in a rented Impala." Oedipa heads out because she needs to sort through her dead lover's business affairs, but during that process she finds cryptic clues about the modern presence of a secret postal system originally set up in the sixteenth century by a man named Tristero, "perhaps a madman, perhaps an honest rebel"—or perhaps a swindler. While Oedipa confronts the endless ways that we are tangled up in networks of miscommunication without ever really knowing each other, I struggled to keep track of players named Pierce Inverarity, Dr. Hilarius, Stanley Koteks, Randy Driblette, Mike Fallopian, and Ghengis Cohen. I hardly knew whether I was thinking too hard or not hard enough, but I eagerly submitted to Tom's kinky perversities without asking him to call me next week or next month so we could talk things through. *Things like, why do I feel dissatisfied and incomplete? How does it really end for Oedipa?*

I found it easy just to melt into the persona of Oedipa as she tries to understand a past that carried her to a present—a review process that's not unlike "watching a movie, just perceptibly out of focus, that the projectionist refused to fix." After all, neither of us is a stranger to the feminine story of waiting for a lover or husband to cause something to happen:

> [She] had also gently conned herself into the curious, Rapunzel-like role of a pensive girl somehow, magically, prisoner among the pines and salt fogs of Kinneret, looking for somebody to say hey, let down your hair. When it turned out to be Pierce she'd happily pulled

out the pins and curlers and down it tumbled in its whispering, dainty avalanche, only when Pierce had got maybe halfway up, her lovely hair turned, through some sinister sorcery, into a great unanchored wig, and down he fell, on his ass. But dauntless, perhaps using one of his many credit cards for a shim, he'd slipped the lock on her tower door and come up the conchlike stairs. . . . But all that had then gone on between them had really never escaped the confinement of that tower.

I now know of critical grumblings about Oedipa's dependent nature failing to support the plausibility of her eventual involvement in a bizarre web of conspiracy. But her initial willingness to be an accessory figure is part of her fascination, speaking to the feminine role offered to and accepted by generations of women. There she is—young, female, and ordinary—anticipating that a man and his money will bring rescue and romance, unaware of how she happens to be locked in a tower, and as yet unaware that she will remain there unless she saves herself.

Pierce sweeps Oedipa off to Mexico City, where she sees a painting of "frail girls with heart-shaped faces, huge eyes, spun-gold hair, prisoners in the top room of a circular tower, embroidering a kind of tapestry which spilled out the slit windows and into the void, seeking hopelessly to fill the void . . . ." Pynchon has noticed that female experience and influence are controlled by imposed walls, and there is little difference between towers. On the fictional canvas, feminine creation spills like water while Oedipa weeps behind her sunglasses, contemplates "the world refracted through those tears," and realizes that neither lover nor location has ended her own imprisonment:

[A]nd so Pierce had taken her away from nothing, there'd been no escape. What did she so desire escape from? Such a captive maiden, having plenty of time

to think, soon realizes that her tower, its height and
architecture, are like her ego only incidental: that what
really keeps her where she is is magic, anonymous
and malignant, visited on her from outside and for no
reason at all.

After that failed love affair, a precarious marriage to a used car
salesman turned disc jockey, and psychotherapy with a shrink interested in studying the effects of LSD on suburban housewives, Oedipa
breaks from the male-determined trajectory of her life and accepts
the challenges of self-determined adventure. Pynchon launches
Everywoman onto the open road where she risks discovery of personal and worldly unknowns— without husband or lover to map the
route—and a feminist role model is created.

1920s Brick Foursquare on Wooded Acre: Suburban Tower?

A long time ago, before I had met Oedipa Maas, "We're fine" rather
than "I'm fine" took shape on my lips and years of brooding would
turn on a pronoun. Having four children and being consumed with
their care, I needed and wanted to be at home with them. And besides, I didn't want to work as a pediatric nurse anymore, didn't want
further proof that in spite of all vigilance and care, Reye's syndrome
and bacterial meningitis and freak falls from bicycles and porches and
countless other things could silence a child—my child—forever. *So
many things can go wrong.* Bike helmets, seat belts, visits to the pediatri-
cian for vaccinations and fevers and stiff necks. Swimming lessons after school because everyone must know how to survive in water. Add
dusting, mopping, washing, ironing, mowing, and weeding to the
daily planner. My family's well-being determined mine; in the name
of love, I consigned myself to the roles of housewife and mother.

I wasn't interested in socializing with two-career couples; I had
nothing to talk about after my specialty—the children's activities—had

been covered. At "required" party appearances, I leaned on humor, often at my own expense, and found mean comfort in noting that the female physicians in our circle of acquaintances were not much fun. (Surely their children could not feel as happy and loved and secure as mine.) Besides, most of those women looked grim or prim in their serious clothes while I worked the smiling, blonde image. *Snug-fitting, midnight blue jersey dress with a bird of paradise painted down the front. Black, Italian leather shoes with spike heels. Long, pale hair curled then brushed then tousled.* But the little voice in my head kept reminding me that those other women looked smart. During one pre-cocktail party dispute, my ego crumbled at my husband's suggestion that if I felt so insecure about adult social events, reading *Newsweek* might give me something to talk about.

Daily life went along relatively unchanged, my children needed me, and my absolute devotion to family deepened. *But could I go on wanting to do what I was doing while still wanting some elusive something else?*

WANTED: SECRET LIFE

Thirty-eight-year-old vanishing woman seeks intellectually challenging work that can be done during school hours. Applicant wishes to escape isolation from public discourse, receive credit for accomplishments, and satisfy desire for just a smidgeon of power. Opportunities for self-esteem building and discovery of meaningful ideas necessary.

During the late 80s, I had found myself oddly receptive to the warning in Toni Morrison's *Beloved*, that love can do harm when it's "'too thick.'" But Sethe, the novel's protagonist who wields a fierce brand of mother-love and may not "know where the world stopped and she began," refuses to loosen her hold: "'Love is or it ain't. Thin love ain't love at all.'" I was flattened with all the thinking that these words generated for me. Did I need to measure each dose of love to ensure that it is warm and alive rather than crazy and smothering? I didn't know the answer, but it seemed that paying attention to the questions nestled within literature might help me figure out how to love and live. So I began with a list of winners—the Booker, Pulitzer, and Nobel prizes for literature during the past few decades—seeking touchstones on a mission of discovery.

I soon realized that something had started that couldn't be stopped. John Berger, Iris Murdoch, Gabriel García Márquez, Nadine Gordimer, Salman Rushdie—I binged on a particular body of work until the craving subsided and released me to take up with the next somebody I fancied during those promiscuous times. As I drifted from my original list, Thomas Hardy, Graham Greene, Chinua Achebe, Vladimir Nabokov, Lawrence Durrell, Margaret Atwood, Thomas Pynchon, Kurt Vonnegut, and Milan Kundera entered my life. And there were others from those blurred book years whose names I've forgotten, but their words fed my restless hunger to know what being alive *means*.

I had become a serious reader, but as time passed, I found that harboring a secret intellectual and imaginative life wasn't enough. I wanted more. I wanted to study literature, try to understand how the authors did what they did on the page, and how they did what they did to me. My own theater full of selves—some lonely, some talking, some laughing, some stumbling, and all of them seemingly real—had been revealed through fiction. I needed people who would talk with me about the ideas and feelings I was discovering; that need (and a shot of courage) finally pushed me to enroll in literature classes at the local community college, just after my fiftieth birthday.

Something else happened. I registered for classes under my full name, Sandra Swinburne. Once classes began, professors and classmates called me "Sandra" and I did not tell them that everyone else on the planet calls me "Sandy." Two selves were out and co-existing: The mother-housewife continued to worry obsessively about her children, and the aspiring adult student willed herself to all but drown in ultra-close readings of the novels she entered. The two looked, spoke, and behaved differently—the student dressing and applying make-up with care; the mother often schlepping around in sweatpants. The student's friends didn't meet the mother's friends, a rule that both simplified and complicated scheduling demands. When signing "Sandra" to school e-mails felt like a sort of forgery, an abbreviated "S" became a compromise with honesty. One body, two selves, and three names fully out and about in the world: The possibilities intrigued me.

Crying Time, Again?

With several literature classes under my belt (and after reading Pynchon's *Vineland* and thinking about reading *Gravity's Rainbow*), I went back to *Crying* because I wanted more of whatever it did to me the first time. But I particularly wanted to understand why I kept replaying the part when Oedipa meets the old man with the "wrecked face, and the terror of eyes gloried in burst veins" slumped in the stairway of a rooming house. When she asks if she can help, he gives her a letter "that looked like he'd been carrying it around for years" and asks her to mail it through the secret mail system to his estranged wife in Fresno. Oedipa takes the letter, but gets woozy at the sight of the man's hopeless life winnowing away before her eyes. She finds herself wanting to feel human connection, to give comfort, yet also to acknowledge realistic limitations:

> Exhausted, hardly knowing what she was doing, she came the last three steps and sat, took the man in her arms, actually held him, gazing out of her smudged eyes down the stairs, back into the morning. She felt wetness against her breast and saw that he was crying again. He hardly breathed but tears came as if being pumped. "I can't help," she whispered, rocking him, "I can't help." It was already too many miles to Fresno.

This reading felt like being at a support group. I could not—cannot—shake that scene; sometimes it makes me cry, and sometimes it stirs me to accept the things in my own life that I cannot fix or control. I cannot choose happiness for people I love, cannot simply will it into being. I must watch my children flounder and grow, accept what I cannot change, and encourage each one to take responsibility for an individual lived life. *Keep talking to me, Tom.*

What's in a Name?

Eight years have not resolved my name juggling, although it recently felt like healthy progress to acknowledge my dilemma to a couple of friends. Afterwards, more thinking about names and roles caused things to mingle and merge, and I started *Crying* from the beginning for the third time: "*One summer afternoon Mrs Oedipa Maas came home from a Tupper*-ware party whose hostess had put perhaps too much kirsch in the fondue to find that she, Oedipa, had been named executor, or she supposed executrix, of the estate of one Pierce Inverarity, a California real estate mogul who had once lost two million dollars in his spare time. . . ." *How am I supposed to read those italics, Tom? Tupper*-ware?

It's a miniscule move to accept that a woman was once involved with a man whose name suggests that he was a lying prick. But *Oedipa*? Why hadn't I worked at decoding Pynchon's plan for that name during prior readings? What does it mean to name a woman—who immediately points out her own diminutive, feminine status as *executrix* rather than *executor*—Oedipa? My problem-solving skills sent me back to Scene One in Sophocles' *Oedipus Rex* where the seer Teresias offers clues about the murderer of former King Laïos: "To the children with whom he lives now he will be / Brother and father—the very same; to her / Who bore him, son and husband—the very same / Who came to his father's bed, wet with his father's blood." Oedipus, King of Thebes, is destroyed by his participation in unknowing patricide and incest; that's the part we all remember, and it doesn't help me understand Pynchon's intent. Oedipa doesn't have children and her parents are non-existent in the novel's time.

Red Herring?

When Oedipa attends a Jacobean revenge play in an attempt to track clues about the alternative mail system, she sits through scenes of torture and treachery delivered by Tristero's minions, and hears of intrigue caused by mother/son and sister/brother incest. But that sidebar of twisted family romance is not enough to explain her name either. *Was this gap in meaning caused by Pynchon's writing or my reading?*

By this time, I was simultaneously re-reading Rilke's *Letters to a Young Poet*, and I began to imagine writing a letter, a correspondence born of frustration:

Dear Tom,

First off, I want to tell you that I'm reading *The Crying of Lot 49* for the third time and I wish you didn't dismiss it as one of your weaker efforts. People may call it your most accessible novel, but I hope that in time you'll stop taking that as an insult because it gives at least one reader plenty to think about.

The real reason that I'm writing is to ask you about why you chose to name your protagonist Oedipa. I read on an internet site that if you write *Sam Spade* on a paper and hold it in front of a mirror to read, it will sound like something close to *Oedipa Maas*. Talk about silly ideas! (I hope that's not why you chose it.) But I suppose it is helpful to think of this character as a detective, boldly sleuthing her way through fantastic conspiracy theories.

I've worked on thinking about the original Oedipus, but I keep hitting the incest wall and can't get past it. Please explain just this one part for now.
Yours truly,
Sandra Swinburne

What about the Questions?

I'm glad that I didn't mail that letter; instead I kept reading and thinking, only harder. Finally, language and literature began to mix through some sort of alchemy, and then I knew. First, Rilke croons advice in his fourth letter:

> Try to love the *questions themselves*, like locked rooms and like books written in a foreign language. Do not now look for the answers. They cannot now be given to you because you could not live them. It is a question of experiencing everything. At present you need to *live* the question. Perhaps you will gradually, without even noticing it, find yourself experiencing the answer, some distant day.

Rilke, younger than a couple of my own children when he wrote these words, sounds wise and patient. *As for me, I think I still love the answers more than the questions.*

As for Oedipus, he tackled the Riddle of the Sphinx, earning this praise from a priest: "You saved us / From the Sphinx, that flinty singer, and the tribute / We paid to her so long; yet you were never / Better informed than we, nor could we teach you: / It was some god breathed in you to set us free." But even more importantly, Oedipus sets out to solve the mystery of why "Thebes is tossed on a murdering sea / And can not lift her head from the death surge." An emissary is sent to Delphi, "Apollo's place of revelation," to discover the cause of their misery and he returns with this advice: "The god commands us to expel from the land of Thebes / An old defilement we are sheltering. / It is a deathly thing, beyond cure; / We must not let it feed upon us longer." Oedipus responds with scattershot questions—"What defilement? How shall we rid ourselves of it?"—and more questions—"Murder of whom? Surely the god has named him?"—and makes a vow: "Then once more I must bring what is dark to light." After all the clues and all the questions, Oedipus finally recalls killing a group of men on the highway, learns that one was his father, and knows the excruciating truth about himself.

How had my brain been so slow, so muddled? Of course the questions are the link. Like Oedipus, Oedipa wades through a morass of questions, refusing to quit, even though difficult truths about her own life come to light. Perhaps Pierce Inverarity designed the clues about a renegade communication network, "some grandiose practical joke he'd cooked up, all for her embarrassment, or terrorizing, or moral improvement." Or perhaps she's crazy; she wonders if all her suspicions about convoluted conspiracies prove that she is "in the cold and sweatless meathooks of a psychosis." Hoping that Dr. Hilarius can explain why she feels so agitated and paranoid about the existence of countless mysteries, Oedipa goes to his clinic only to find him armed with a rifle and making faces that he once used during his internship in Buchenwald. He advises her to "'cherish'" any fantasy that she may have: "'Hold it tightly by its little tentacle, don't let the Freudians coax it away or the pharmacists poison it out of you. Whatever it is, hold it dear, for when you lose it you go over by that much to the others. You begin to cease to be.'" *Oddly enough, Hilarius offers a suggestion not unlike Rilke's: Cherish your fantasies; love the questions.*

A visit to Mucho Maas proves to Oedipa that the defining role implied in the name "Mrs Oedipa Maas" has lost relevance: Her husband is becoming "less himself and more generic" with the help of LSD pills prescribed by Dr. Hilarius. Mucho no longer remembers the things that worried him, like the frightening dreams about the used car lot where he once worked: "'We were a member of the National Automobile Dealers' Association. N.A.D.A. Just this creaking metal sign that said nada, nada, against the blue sky. I used to wake up hollering.'" Mucho feels relief at no longer caring about what his own life means, and he can't help Oedipa.

Pynchon's Everywoman is on her own, so full of questions and paranoia about sinister power schemes and clandestine communication networks that her teeth ache and dark voices take over the audio of her dreams: "Your gynecologist has no test for what she was pregnant with." Despite overwhelming evidence that truth can torment, Oedipa keeps driving into the unknown "with the courage you find you have when there is nothing more to lose." The "Tristero 'forgeries'" from Pierce's stamp collection are to be auctioned as "lot 49" and Oedipa wants to know who's interested in them. Entering the auction site, she meets philatelist Genghis Cohen who greets her with authoritative posturing about the stamp world. With the growing confidence of a woman who has found her own way out of the tower, Oedipa informs Cohen: "'Your fly is open.'"

Metaphor: The Last Act?

The Crying of Lot 49 has a spell on me. Why else would I read it three times and still feel there is more to learn, that I'm missing something? I suppose my own need for answers comes into play, but postmodern Pynchon avoids conclusions and never reveals what finally happens to Oedipa. I wish I knew how her story ends because it might hold clues about what happens to the me of the three names and burgeoning number of selves. That wondering causes me to conjure other Dear Tom letters in which I earnestly try to explain the flickering agitation of not knowing, but I never send them.

My children are grown now and sometimes ask for my support and advice, but I've tried to accept that I often can't help them, can't make their lives less complicated, and can't lighten their worries.

The Last Good Obsession

Scraggly gardens cast a brooding shadow over my house, dirt mottles windows, dog hair and cat fur tumble across hardwood, papers and books clutter tables—in part because I no longer care much about those surfaces. Instead, I read, I write, I think, and, now and then, I look forward to socializing with two-career couples. When asked at a party, "How are you?" I might answer, "We're fine," but that's because some of my selves enjoy a few glasses of Cabernet and sometimes find themselves enjoying each other's company after having drunk too many for the one body.

Oddly enough, I'm suddenly interesting to those lifer-professionals who slump under too familiar jobs. At a recent gathering, next to a silver tray of poached salmon, a female physician wearing a smart, black suit confided to me that she wishes she could love her work, wishes she could find something to do that makes her happy, wishes she could imagine a way to endure the loneliness that awaits her when her youngest daughter leaves for college in the fall. She said she envies my belated discoveries about reading and writing—apparently unaware of the selves and names that bicker behind my façade, obviously not understanding that my destination remains unknown. The sad and serious doctor focused on wanting solutions for her own discontent, and I did not tell her that I mostly deal in questions. Instead, I smiled knowingly and pretended to be way happier than I am.

Maybe I should have told her that there are clues buried in *The Crying of Lot 49*, that "[t]he act of metaphor then was a thrust at truth and a lie, depending where you were: inside, safe, or outside, lost. Oedipa did not know where she was." Maybe I should have told her that eventually she would need to head out alone on the open road.

Faulkner's Lover

It was as if she knew somehow that time was short, that
autumn was almost upon her, without knowing yet
the exact significance of autumn.
—William Faulkner, *Light in August*

My last good obsession began in the splintered light of a snow-covered January during my fiftieth year. By February, I was nearly out of my mind because he was so completely in it; he could be everywhere, framing anything. Four tumultuous years would pass before I could enter my bed without reaching for him. And even now, the littlest thing happens and I'm reminded of a desire or a phrase that can turn a certain way only between us. I still want to gaze into his thoughts so we can remember together. Never old, never stale, he surprises me each time as if it is the first. When he suggests concealed notes—even traps—I toss reason aside. I want to taste those "forbidden wordsymbols" that still shock and excite me, knowing that in the end I will be like so many other women: "'Whether they are seventeen or fortyseven, when they finally come to surrender completely, it's going to be in words.'"

In what seems like a prior existence, I had not yet imagined that an intellectually creative life that can sometimes creep about in public was possible for me because I was immersed in worrying my children into young adulthood. My external life was peopled by whip-smart boys laughing around the kitchen table while they waited for my pumpkin-pecan or strawberry pie to appear, and clever girls who raided my closet for costume party clothes, looking for silk blouses and pencil skirts that would temporarily transform them into the secretaries they'd never be. Then they began to leave me in waves; every couple of years another child neared eighteen and received college acceptance letters, as did his or her friends. Three times into those celebrations of possibility for people I love, I cradled my losses and began to wonder what I would do after the inevitable departure of my fourth and last child. *What about my external life then? What about the coming quiet?*

It was as if I needed Outward Bound. So for my fiftieth birthday, I drove alone to Cape Cod to spend a week with my nineteen-year-old daughter who was ready to quit a summer job in a laboratory. Forty hours a week, she drained blue plasma from horseshoe crabs (a quantity that they can spare, theoretically) in order to harvest their magical *Limulus amebocyte lysate.* These primitive creatures do not have a developed immune system; instead they have LAL on tap to arrest invading infectious agents by forming a clot around them. When used in medical tests for humans, LAL can help diagnose infections or detect contamination in things like vaccine serum because of that clotting mechanism. My vegetarian child believes in the importance of these medical uses, but she worried that the donors were being harmed in spite of scientific assurance that they were not, so she was done puncturing crabs with large-bored needles. For her final five days as a lab technician, I drove her to work, sometimes going in to see the clueless creatures piled in plastic garbage cans in the waiting area, and then went to the beach for sun and waves. Every afternoon I strolled around the town of Woods Hole and stopped at a café called Pie in the Sky for iced tea and one or two pastries from the eye-popping assortment splayed within a glass case.

The Last Good Obsession

Walking along the shore one evening, my daughter and I stopped to watch a small rainbow parachute sail across cloudless blue while a little human form dangled beneath it. A rope was stretched from the seemingly weightless marionette to a speeding boat that careened through the water in front of us. I who am afraid of heights experienced respectful awe; my daughter who is afraid of heights felt longing. I said something like, "Oh, my God!" but she said, "All summer I've wanted to parasail even though it looks scary. Two people can go together, so my roommate and I talked about doing it before we left here, even though it costs a lot. Then she went home before we ever got up the nerve or the money."

Without waiting to think, I blurted out, "Let's do it! You and I can go and I'll pay." I suppose I didn't need to think at that moment because I'd been thinking for months: *What am I going to do?* I had recently read a quote credited to Native American culture in a magazine at my doctor's office, where I was waiting to be seen for banging headaches: "If you are afraid of life there is no joy." A voice in my troubled head had taken up that warning and wouldn't let go of it, even though I seemed unable to respond in deed. There on the beach, something had happened. Perhaps the stars were trying to speak: I wanted to parasail.

I could try to impress upon you how frightened I felt when a couple of days later I handed my credit card to the speedboat driver who would launch my daughter and me on a tandem ride toward heaven's door. Or I could prattle on about how vast the ocean looked, how wild the wind felt as it swept through my hair, and how we joked about the skirt of my mom-swimsuit being anchored so that it wouldn't flip up over my head while we skimmed through the air. Or I could paint a scene of two women, one just beginning and one nearer ending, as they giggled and gasped when the boat gradually slowed, dipped them into the ocean, then hit full throttle to send them soaring upward again. But that's only what it was, not what it *meant.* The actual parasailing was most importantly a ticket to the next adventure and the next. The courage was the thing, the transformative body current that nudged a hesitant mind onto a plane where risks became possible. Before my navy-with-little-white-flowers swimsuit was dry, I wanted to try other challenges; I needed to get out into the world.

Early in my tenure as a stay-at-home-mom, I had adopted the belief that books were an essential part of good parenting. I bought classic and prize-winning children's books that my husband and I read aloud to our children even after each had learned to read alone. I went so far as to institute the Books for Money program during their elementary school years: Read twenty, age-appropriate books over summer vacation and earn twenty dollars of mad money. This brainstorm to promote reading could have backfired, but it didn't.

I had also figured out midstream in my own journey that the ideas harbored within books could both sustain and change me. The emotional and intellectual life I found in literature tumbled and grew until I found that my identity as an adult reader defined me in ways that I needed. Jude and Sue tore at each other's clothes while I ironed, and Billy Pilgrim and I escaped reality by playing Cinderella while I pushed the lawn mower. My stock rose among a few people in the neighborhood when I began recommending William Wharton's *Birdy*, and Garp's troubles carried me through more than one awkward cocktail party.

Returning from Cape Cod, I talked myself into enrolling in fall semester literature classes—mythology and women's lit—at a community college. I happily sank into *The Odyssey*, added *The Iliad* out of pure curiosity, and couldn't get my fill of Helen and Paris, Agamemnon and Clytemnestra, and the temperamental crew on Mount Olympus. Tantrists, sibyls, Apache Vagina Girls, anchorites in cells, and angels in the house. With my mind whirling, news of Lilith was the last straw: How could I have reached the age of fifty and not heard rumors about Adam's defiant first wife? What else had I missed?

When a packet arrived in the mail stating that I had been recommended for honors classes, I shopped through and decided I would try the Faulkner seminar during spring semester since I'd always skipped over him, in spite of seeing his name on various book lists that shaped my reading life. After I registered, a note arrived from the professor suggesting that students read one of the books on the syllabus to get a feel for Faulkner before classes began the end of January. I went with *Light in August* because a copy of it stamped "Property of Brighton High School" had found its way onto the living room bookshelf. I didn't ask; I just started reading Faulkner.

———

Outside of Jefferson, Mississippi, Joe Christmas asks a passing boy about the big house shrouded in tangled trees and shrubbery. "'That where Miz Burden stay at,'" he answers, and further probing yields, "'Aint nobody live there but her.'" So Christmas waits; he lies in the dark amidst the overgrowth studying the house, watches the light from a kerosene lamp in an upstairs window, and still waits after the light goes out. He's aware of his body against the earth, "groin, hip, belly, breast, forearms," and he's aware of his hunger. Upon rising, he finds the kitchen at the back of the house, takes notice of the door and "would have found it unlocked if he had tried it." He chooses a window and finds that it "was even open, propped up with a stick. 'What do you think about that,' he thought." He moves through the dark room, guided by his senses, toward the aroma of peas and molasses. When he hears "the soft sound of slippered feet," he waits, and soon he sees Joanna Burden by candlelight, her face "quiet, grave, utterly unalarmed." When she speaks, it is to say, "'If it is just food you want, you will find that.'"

But it's more than food he wants. Joe struggles with emotional damage from a childhood spent in an orphanage and foster care. Having been labeled an unwanted child of mixed race, he wields his imagined black blood like a club against authority, women, and himself. As a young man on the move, he allows his shame and anger to surface when he visits white prostitutes but is unable to pay for their services; the trick is to tell them he's a negro, counting on their disgust at having had sex with him to facilitate his escape. So when Joe sees Joanna in that whisper of light, a woman alone in a nice house, he decides to have her by rape because "there had opened before him, instantaneous as a landscape in a lightningflash, a horizon of physical security and adultery if not pleasure."

Joanna loses her virginity in a "hard, untearful and unselfpitying and almost manlike yielding of that surrender." Afterwards Joe reflects that it had been "as if he struggled physically with another man for an object of no actual value to either, and for which they struggled on principle alone," or perhaps that "'it was like I was the woman and she was the man.'" Dissatisfied with his perceived role in this accounting, he re-enters the house the next night, goes to her unlocked bedroom, and repeats the act, tearing at her clothes and "talking to her, in a tense, hard, low voice." But she does not respond as he expects: "It was almost as though she were helping him." Joe feels rage rather than passion, and Joanna's body "might have been the body of a dead woman not yet stiffened." He assumes that through sexual violence he has "'made a woman of her at last,'" and that she hates him.

Instead, Joanna loans Joe a cot to sleep on in the cabin near the house. By light of day, he guesses that she is "better than thirtyfive," but in fact she's better than forty. With all of her immediate relatives dead, Joanna has lived alone for twenty years. By day, she counsels black women who come to her for advice, and she writes replies to the administrators and students of negro schools and colleges that seek her support. She wears plain house dresses, keeps her hair pinned up (sometimes covering it with "a cloth sunbonnet like a countrywoman"), and wears spectacles while working at her "scarred, rolltop desk." And each night, she retires to her spinster's bed—until Joe enters, and she sees in him an opportunity to change her life.

Baffled by Joanna and by himself, Joe Christmas admits, "'My God. How little I know about women, when I thought I knew so much.'" The next night he finds the door unlocked and food waiting, as if she *expects* him. Joe throws the dishes, leaves the house, and stays away for months. Returning to the cabin one September evening, he finds Joanna waiting there to talk, to tell him about events leading up to this moment in her life, and to lure him back to her bed. Joe studies her and decides: "'She's trying to be a woman and she dont know how.'"

I was dazzled by *Light in August*. Human failings, sometimes despicable and sometimes just plain sad, pile on at every turn, yet hope glimmers through now and then to carry the weary into the next hour or the next day. And even though Joanna Burden does not appear until halfway through the book, she was the character who got to me. Why isn't she defeated by that sexual assault? Why did I so willingly suspend my own values and find her relationship with Joe Christmas not only provocative but a good idea? I wanted her to leave the window open, wanted her solitude to be broken. Something at a primal level made me want more, more plundering the dark troves of eroticism and despair that wait on and under the skin, more thrumming of words into perverse twists of imagery—more Faulkner. I couldn't wait for class to begin.

Fewer than twenty students gathered for the three-hour Monday night seminar. The professor was an earnest sixty-year-old man who loved American literature, especially *Moby Dick* and all things Faulkner. The plan was that each week we would read one of Faulkner's novels and submit a journal response, all the while working toward a final thesis project and presentation. Somebody in class talked about being interested in Faulkner's use of "the gothic"; I didn't know what that meant.

Feeling too unsure of myself to talk in class, I poured everything onto the page. Our first assignment was to read *The Unvanquished* and

I imagined being Drusilla, a woman who demonstrates her refusal of the genteel, Southern lady role by wearing pants, cutting her hair short, and carrying a gun. But Drusilla also knows how to use sexuality for persuasion, and does. My January 29, 2001 journal refers to the scene in which she tries to convince her stepson Bayard to kill the man responsible for his father's death: "Then she came to me, melted as women will and can, the arms with the wrist-and elbow-power to control horses about my shoulder. . . . I thought then of the woman of thirty, the symbol of the ancient and eternal Snake. . . ." The befuddled boy decides against murder, and resists the possibilities promised by Drusilla's body, but their story is taut with the tension of desire. Faulkner's Yoknapatawpha County was where I wanted to be as I wrote, "Sex, death, and damnation: I think Faulkner is interested in these and so are we."

By February 5, my journal response murmurs faint resistance to a growing fascination: "I am a little worried about slipping into a Faulkner-induced madness!" And by February 12, having just finished *Go Down, Moses,* I blurt out, "He is breaking my heart," and then follow with a quote from a male character defeated by a life of slavery: "'Whar's ourn?' he cried. 'Whar's mine?'" But these excerpts can only hint at the emotional content of what I wrote, because each week I submitted at least ten typed pages of exploratory response that took increasingly daring bites out of Faulkner's versions of sex, death, and damnation. By the time we reached *Light in August* as a class, the professor seemed anxious, admitted to having trouble sleeping after Monday night seminars, and admitted that, like Faulkner, he drank too much.

———

Sitting on the cot in the cabin, Joanna tells Joe that she was raised in the convictions of her grandfather, Calvin Burden, who had been cast under a spell of ancestral fire and brimstone that he later modified with a dose of mystical Spanish Catholicism. Grandfather Burden believed that slavery had literally stained the black race, and that by ending the bondage, both blacks and whites would be freed from damnation. Joanna's father passes the legacy of these beliefs to her half-brother (also named Calvin) and to her. When the psychological load of responsibility for an entire race overwhelms her, Joanna asks to be released, but her father demands that she must "'rise, you must raise the shadow with you'"—or be cursed. Sharing this information frames an intimacy between Joe and Joanna, and he finds that her voice is "almost gentle now."

An altered dynamic characterizes the next phase of their relationship, during which Joe can no longer pretend to have any control over their union: "It was as though he had fallen into a sewer." After all the repression and wasted years, Joanna is obsessed by desires, as if determined to make a woman of herself according to a forbidden mold, and she needs Joe as both participant and witness. She wants words, wants to tell Joe about her day, and insists that he reciprocate. But she also wants other words that signify her sexual awakening: "She had an avidity for the forbidden wordsymbols; an insatiable appetite for the sound of them on his tongue and her own. She revealed the terrible and impersonal curiosity of a child about forbidden subjects and objects; that rapt and tireless and detached interest of a surgeon in the physical body and its possibilities."

With "an unexpected and infallible instinct for intrigue," Joanna creates a Mississippi tableau seemingly inspired by visions of Sodom and Gomorrah. She hides notes for Joe, traps him in a scripted web, and sometimes surprises him with a demand to find her "hidden, in closets, in empty rooms, waiting, panting, her eyes in the dark glowing like the eyes of cats." She instructs him to meet her for "trysts beneath certain shrubs about the grounds, where he would find her naked, or with her clothing half torn to ribbons upon her, in the wild throes of nymphomania. . . ." Unrestrained by the walls of her ancestors, Joanna breaks societal taboos and seeks ecstasy in the forbidden, "her wild hair, each strand of which would seem to come alive like octopus tentacles, and her wild hands and her breathing: 'Negro! Negro! Negro!'"

Joanna "was completely corrupted," and Joe Christmas "began to be afraid." Obsessed by imagination, she becomes like "two creatures that struggled in the one body like two moon-gleamed shapes struggling drowning in alternate throes upon the surface of a black thick pool beneath the last moon." She's been alone too long, alone through twenty years of lonely nights, and knows that the man who came in through the kitchen window is her last chance at a full life. Under the threatening "shadow of autumn," Joanna wills herself to experience more womanliness and more life: She tells Joe that she is pregnant, adding, "'A full measure. Even to a bastard negro child. I would like to see father's and Calvin's faces.'"

Finding that the notion of a child is still not enough, Joanna channels her energy into a scheme that would transform Joe: "'Do you realize,' she said, 'that you are wasting your life?'" She first proposes that he take over her business with the negro schools, and later specifies that he can attend school on her recommendation, perhaps to study law with her own negro lawyer, Mr. Peebles. Joe avoids her, and he can't stop thinking about her.

When Joe comprehends that Joanna expects him to acknowledge his presumed black blood in public, he attacks with words: "'You're old. I never noticed that before. An old woman. You've got gray in your hair.'" He hits her with his fist, tells her that there's never been a baby, and then speaks "the words which she had once loved to hear on his tongue, which she used to say that she could taste there, murmurous obscene, caressing." Lying across the bed with her mouth bleeding, Joanna admits the lure of death.

Seeking reconciliation with her God, Joanna begins to pray behind locked doors, and when she allows Joe to enter, she badgers him to pray for salvation as well. But he refuses, and they remain at a stalemate: "And they would stand for a while longer in the quiet dusk peopled, as though from their loins, by a myriad ghosts of dead sins and delights, looking at one another's still and fading face, weary, spent, and indomitable." Finally, Joanna says, "'Then there's just one other thing to do.'" On the night when she holds a revolver containing two bullets under her shawl, and Joe holds his straight-edged razor, she calls for her last light in August: "'Light the lamp.'"

———

He was my lamp and I couldn't get enough of him. I wanted only the honey rhythm of his words oozing through me as I struggled to shape the next phase of my own life. I began to imagine that I was Faulkner's lover.

None of my fascination with the Joe and Joanna saga is intended as an argument in praise of rape, but rather as an attempt to understand need and desire that plunge into obsession and beyond. For reasons very different from Joanna's, I felt limited by the house of my childhood, a house containing few books (other than the ivory and black bound volumes of *The World Book Encyclopedia*) in a small town next to a school building that accommodated kindergarten through twelfth-grade students from surrounding farm country. I have one book left from those early years, *Little Women*, and I do not recall receiving any others.

Trying to prop open a window, I had begun reading as an adult to educate myself through literature. But I wanted more than a self-improvement hobby; I wanted expertise that might silence the disparaging inner commentary—*not good enough, not smart enough*—that had subdued me for so long. I needed a space where my own imagination and words could tackle big ideas about life and death without the tethers of my provincial past. In my growing passion for all things Faulkner, I was looking for clues about where intellectually creative endeavors might take me in the outside world, but I also wanted, impossibly, the man who could have said those forbidden words to me.

As the seminar group worked through the Faulkner syllabus, each book generated more questions that I needed to pursue. I found evidence of both Christian and Gnostic teachings in "The Old People" when Sam Fathers, an old man of mixed blood who is both wise and receptive to nature's ways, takes young Isaac McCaslin into the wilderness to hunt, and more importantly to teach him about man's place in creation. Faulkner introduces this story with an echo from Genesis, "At first there was nothing," then shows that mankind's choices begin with a gift made manifest: "Then the buck was there. He did not come into sight; he was just there, looking not like a ghost but as if all of light were condensed in him and he were the source of it, not only moving in it but disseminating it, already running, seen first as you always see the deer, in that split second after he has already seen you. . . ." Sam tells the boy when to shoot, narrates the ritual for cutting the buck's throat, then put his fingers into "the hot smoking blood and wiped them back and forth across the boy's face."

The buck was mesmeric. What about living in nature with honor and humility and spirituality? *Show me the thread to follow through the labyrinth.* Sam believes that the glowing buck is provided and meant to be taken according to a wilderness ritual that allows man to eat and live. Certain Christian Eucharist ceremonies proclaim, "Take, eat; this is my body" to remind the faithful that Christ died so that they might live spiritually. Meanwhile, Gnostics imagined a metaphor for the divine source of *being* as light particles, some of which are trapped within earthly creations; so humans must seek knowledge, learn the truth of their origin, before they may reunite their light with God's light.

I wanted to understand Faulkner's interest in embodiment and light, so I read John Dart's *The Laughing Savior*—its title a reference to the Gnostic belief that Christ did not actually suffer the crucifixion because he had already left the flesh that hung on the cross and watched from a distance, laughing at man's lack of knowledge. Then I envisioned Sam Fathers as a vessel of light particles: Knowing the

The Last Good Obsession

Chickasaw words of his ancestors, knowing the light in the buck, and knowing the truth of origin, his earthly life is complete.

Reading "The Bear," I am there when Lion, the dog with an untamable spirit, attacks and is caught by Old Ben, the bear who reigns over the wilderness but faces death with the mauled dog "in both arms, almost loverlike." I am there when Boon, a man still so natural that he resists civilizing influences and loves Lion more than anything, tackles the bear and drives his knife into its heart hoping to save the dog. *My whole being blown open, Faulkner and I "almost loverlike" holding Boon and Lion and Old Ben, all of us clutching and clinging, asking which is which, dancing and asking, How can we know? How can we know?*

But when the bear falls in an honorable death and Sam Fathers collapses as well, having "'just quit,'" my flight of rapture ends. I am there when Sam waits for his own death, "'Let me out, master.... Let me go home,'" and when he instructs Boon and young Isaac about final preparations for his return to the source of all life. I, a long-lapsed Catholic, wanted to pray out of sheer spiritual wonder.

Because of Sam Fathers' compelling enlightenment, I began to think that Buddhism might teach me something about the sort of living and dying Faulkner had in mind while writing about him. So I read *The Tibetan Book of Living and Dying* by Sogyal Rinpoche and latched onto a lilting description that captures the rightness in Sam's departure: "[W]hat happens at the moment of death, for everyone, is this: The Ground Luminosity ['fundamental, inherent nature'] dawns in vast splendor, and with it brings an opportunity for total liberation— if, and only if, you have learned how to recognize it." From beyond the grave, Faulkner was leading me through an emotional wilderness of my own. His insistence on a continuum of deep knowledge that binds man with nature through time clouded my eyes with a faraway look. When asked about my consuming fascination with Faulkner, I made light of it, answered that I was just listening to the voices. The truth was that I was listening to only one voice, *his* voice.

Faulkner's Sam Fathers had taken me to places within myself that I hadn't known existed. I felt so grateful for the journey that I bought another copy of *The Tibetan Book of Living and Dying* and gave it to the seminar professor as a thank you gift. I took it to class and approached him at the desk during break to say: "You showed me Sam Fathers; maybe there's something in this book for you." He looked stunned and then began waving the book around, explaining to anyone left in the room that I'd given it him, *given it to him*. I thought that perhaps I shouldn't have.

I continued to write about Faulkner like a zealot: If I could understand his words, I might understand my own life. In class, I listened and took notes with an intensity that must have puzzled the other students. Sometimes I'd practice in my head what I wanted to say about a book, if only I could find the courage to raise my hand. I was near bursting with ideas that I'd jot in the margins of my notebook to use as prompts, but the weight of shyness and raw emotion kept me silent. The professor looked my way too often, knowing and waiting for something to happen; there were times when class discussion drifted aimlessly and he would look at me and ask: "What do *you* think?" He knew only too well that my thoughts were in troubled territory. I was so besotted by Faulkner that I couldn't sleep. I started sneaking cigarettes after several years of abstinence, looked to John Donne for sensuous links between body and spirit, and even tried reading *Zarathustra*. I wanted to study Buddhism, I wanted to go deer hunting, I wanted to live in Mississippi.

As I Lay Dying took me stumbling through Addie Bundren's hatred of life—"my father used to say that the reason for living was to get ready to stay dead a long time"—and provoked a weird affinity for crazy Darl, "with his eyes gone further than the food and the lamp, full of the land dug out of his skull and the holes filled with distance beyond the land." Faulkner worries the precarious link of mind and body through Darl—"How do our lives ravel out into the no-wind, no-sound, the weary gestures wearily recapitulant: echoes of

The Last Good Obsession

old compulsions with no-hand on no-strings: in sunset we fall into fu-
rious attitudes, dead gestures of dolls"—and I worried as well. When
Darl refers to himself in the third person, "Darl has gone to Jackson.
They put him on the train, laughing, down the long car laughing. . . ,"
I wondered about Faulkner's interest in playing with a Freudian deck.
By 1930, when Darl appears in print, twenty-one years had passed
since Freud arrived to lecture in America, so I bought *Beyond the Pleasure
Principle* and *Civilization and Its Discontents*, and skimmed through them
looking for clues about what Faulkner knew.

Then I found R. D. Laing's study of schizophrenia, *The Divided
Self*, and read about "a mind more or less tenuously linked to a body,"
and feelings of "despairing aloneness." But the most satisfying, albeit
non-scientific, explanation for what shapes Darl appears in *Love's Body*
by Norman O. Brown: "Schizophrenics are suffering from the truth."

I was the Romantic moth fluttering at Faulkner's flame. Sometimes
as I wrote about him during sleepless nights, my prose went dreamy,
like the flights of a woman in love. Responding to *Sanctuary* on March
12, I wrote: "Temple drifts out of her body, escaping the current version of reality which has insinuated itself upon her," and then "P.S. I
am still trying to understand what it is about Faulkner's writing that
turns the reading of it into obsession." Another burst on March 13 resulted in "I know that Faulkner is saying something for the first time,
and he chose me." My adventurous essays came back from the professor with notations scratched in the margins: "Wow!" and "What
a writer!" and "I'm learning so much from your thinking!" During
class, with each of his hesitant looks my way, I felt like he was sliding
into my eyes to ask if there was room for him in the spell I was under.

By the time I finished *The Hamlet* with Eula Varner inhabiting
"too much of mammalian female meat" and Ike Snopes stalking the
cow he passionately loves, I felt totally nuts. I needed a break from
Faulkner. One night I purposely took Goethe into my bed to break
the grip of a compulsive monogamy: I was going to cheat with *The
Sorrows of Young Werther.*

Sandra Swinburne

Goethe's epistolary novel begins with a letter written by Werther and dated May 4, 1771: "I can't tell you how glad I am to have got away. Dear friend, how strange is the human heart!" So far, so good; this spoke to me and it was a change from Faulkner, Faulkner, Faulkner. On May 10, Werther seems delighted by nature and inordinately absorbed with himself: "My whole being is filled with a marvelous gaiety, like the sweet spring mornings that I enjoy with all my heart." I began to doubt my taste in men, but I kept going:

> When the mists in my beloved valley steam all around me; when the sun rests on the surface of the impenetrable depths of my forest at noon and only single rays steal into the inner sanctum; when I lie in the tall grass beside a rushing brook and become aware of the remarkable diversity of a thousand little growing things on the ground, with all their peculiarities; when I can feel the teeming of a minute world amid the blades of grass and the innumerable, unfathomable shapes of worm and insect closer to my heart and . . . .

Wait a minute. Mists, brook, grass, bugs. . . . I've been here before! I've seen this valley—and that's when a blur of Goethe/Faulkner hit. I threw aside my quilt and stomped down the stairs to retrieve *The Hamlet* with its Ike Snopes passages. Faulkner and I were going to have it out, line by line. I was the one who was supposed to be cheating and now it seemed like someone else had been seduced by the words of another as well.

In a section titled "The Long Summer: Chapter One," Faulkner uses elevated prose to narrate the story of Ike, an idiot who lives by instinct rather than intellect and loves a cow. Ike's pastoral idyll with his beloved begins when he hurries from the barn through "the growing visibility, the gradation from gray through primrose to the morning's ultimate gold, to the brow of the final hill, to let himself downward into the creekside mist and lie in the drenched myriad waking life of grasses and listen for her approach."

My intention had been to feel less crazy by escaping Faulkner and I couldn't; lying next to a babbling brook with Werther, I had been hurtled back to my voyeuristic experience with Ike Snopes. With darting eyes and galloping pulse, I underlined parallel phrases and images in each text. On May 12, Werther describes watching young girls collect water from a spring and imagines seeing "our forefathers meeting and courting at wells like this." *Hmmm.* I returned to Ike, who waits in a state of sensory alert near the water's edge: "Then he would hear her, coming down the creekside in the mist. It would not be after one hour, two hours, three; the dawn would be empty, the moment and she would not be, then he would hear her and he would lie drenched in the wet grass, serene and one and indivisible in joy, listening to her approach." Even before he sees her, "the whole mist reeked with her," and he is transfixed. "He would lie amid the waking instant of earth's teeming minute life, the motionless fronds of water-heavy grasses stooping into the mist before his face in black, fixed curves. . . ."

I noticed that just as Werther waxes euphorically about his capers during the merry days of May, Ike's trysts with his beloved cow cause him to travel "beneath the May noon," and "the sleight hand of May shapes them both." Then, after I got control of my sleuthing compulsions so I could continue with Goethe, I discovered that Werther nurses an obsessive and forbidden love for a married woman named Lotte. But unlike Ike's naive delight in the sheer splendor of his cow, Werther's high-brow love is self-absorbed and manipulative. Had my man Bill shaped a story of obsessive (although bestial) love in Mississippi around Goethe's story of a dandy fixated on the acrobatics of his own heart as an inspired parody? Consciously? Unconsciously? Sam Fathers' plea coursed through me: *Let me out. . . .*

During the closing weeks of spring semester, I prepared a final paper and presentation about the mind/body scissions found in the Faulkner texts that we'd studied. Yet as I worked, I knew the next thing to do: I applied for admission to graduate school, aiming toward a Master of Arts degree in literature so I could continue studying Faulkner. I asked my seminar professor to write a recommendation and, already inside my eyes, he answered that he would be happy to do that. Trying to defuse the tension between us, I only half-jokingly said, "Don't tell them I'm crazy." The following week he gave me a copy of his letter anointing me "the best student I have had in my thirty-three years of teaching," and an acceptance into the program soon followed.

I began my graduate studies with a summer course in postmodern literature where a surly professor tested my shaky self-confidence. Then I signed up for Chaucer, English Romantics (because Keats was one of Faulkner's favorites), and a course on writer's craft (which gave me new ideas about my future). Part way through the semester I met with the graduate advisor to discuss requirements, and he eventually got around to asking about my interests for a final thesis project. By then I had noticed several Lilith references scattered through Faulkner's work, and I was dead set that I would research their significance. But when I explained my intention, he told me there wasn't anyone among the current faculty working on Faulkner, and that I "should consider plan B." I boldly and uncharacteristically stated that there would be no alternate plan; I would find a suitable mentor.

By spring of 2002, the professor from postmodern literature had agreed to mentor my master's thesis, I was immersed in three more courses, and had registered for the Yoknapatawpha Conference in Oxford, Mississippi. I figured that the July Faulkner fest would be an opportunity for me to hear presentations and fill off hours with library research for my thesis. As my intellectual life grew by persistent, academic leaps, I noticed that the romantic throes of Faulkner fixation had cooled; however, I had begun calling my thesis "The Dead Lover Project."

The Last Good Obsession

My time in Mississippi was another sort of Outward Bound experience. I flew to Memphis, rented a car, and drove through long stretches of swampland with a map on my lap until I found Ole Miss. The campus looked as I had imagined, somehow stubborn and grand, and I could scarcely believe that I was there. When I entered the main conference room, there on an easel up front was a portrait of Bill, looking like the man from my dreams. Little did I know that two days later I would stand next to him for a photograph, graze the upper edge of his frame with my shoulder, and hear a crash as he hit the floor, taking a large potted plant with him. I sat down, rattled and embarrassed by the spectacle, while the janitorial staff cleaned up.

When I tackled the library, I explained to the librarians that although I was oldish in years, I was newish to research skills. They helped me pry into databases looking for scholarly material about Lilith, and looked disappointed that nobody had published work focused specifically on Faulkner's fascination with Adam's mythical first wife. But I was thrilled; Lilith in Mississippi was mine. Faulkner and I know that desire is a troubling thing, and I wanted to write about how he showed this over and over again as his repressed male characters get involved with rebellious, sexual women like Joanna Burden, Caddy Compson, Eula Varner, and Charlotte Rittenmeyer.

Before leaving Mississippi, I sat under a tree next to Faulkner's grave and felt like crying, and I drove to the little town of New Albany where he was born. Visiting Rowan Oak, the house where he lived with his wife and daughter, I saw the stable that I know from photographs, Mammy Callie Barr's house out back, and his study with *The Fable* famously plotted out in black ink across its white walls. I asked the caretaker if there was a restroom, and I was directed to a not modernized bathroom on the first floor of the main house. Looking at the old white seat, I considered my dislike for public toilets, my concerns about cleanliness and germs, and my habit of unrolling toilet paper to spread across the seat before sitting. *But this is Bill's house.* Without further hesitation, I unzipped and dropped my pants to use Faulkner's toilet.

After returning home, I continued course work and took off on my Faulkner research. I re-read the novels I knew, read the lesser novels because I wanted his full body of work seeping through me, his essays and letters, his stories, and an assortment of biographies. Then I picked a path through Lilith myth to document manifestations of her troublesome presence in the Old Testament, Kabbalah, and on ancient artifacts. I wrote and wrote about Lilith as one of Faulkner's tickets into the perils of desire, and when I stopped my thesis existed as proof that, like Joanna Burden, I had opened windows and changed my life.

———

Upstairs in my house there's a room where visitors are not welcome. One long wall is filled by bookshelves, while the others are lined with contiguous French windows that open inward by tarnished brass handles. My scarred desk sits in front of one of these windows so I can worry the highest branches of a gnarled silver maple that rises through the ever-changing light. I go there to write, with him resting on the shelves at my back. Sometimes I turn to look or to touch a spine not cold amidst the dust, knowing that he's there, as surely as Homer Baron lies waiting for Miss Emily Grierson on the bridal bed of her dreams.

I've moved on outwardly, and a parade of others has passed through my bed as I seek those who can urge me with words to think about the varied manifestations of life among the living. Sometimes, though, I simply sit in there with him, twirling a strand of my gray hair now colored red and remembering a lament from *The Unvanquished*: "[A]nd I realised then the immitigable chasm between all life and all print—that those who can, do, those who cannot and suffer enough because they cant, write about it."

Perhaps the Last Time

> She shut her eyes: the sweet word "promiscuity"
> came to her mind and suffused her; she enunciated
> silently to herself: "promiscuity of ideas."
> —Milan Kundera, *Identity*

I lay nearly motionless on a four-poster bed in a Savannah hotel. My husband and I had just returned from a restaurant made famous on the Cooking Channel where we'd shared mounds of corn bread and biscuits, bacon-wrapped shrimp, and chicken potpie. Add a couple glasses of wine and split a slice of pecan pie and my stomach hurt more than it had in a long time. I silently vowed that I would never again surrender so completely to temptation, knowing that my word was good for a day or two at best. On my back and moving only one finger, I flicked a page of Milan Kundera's novel *Identity*. "'Men don't turn to look at me anymore,'" Chantal laments. Perhaps it was just bad timing to read that, feeling as I did while my husband concentrated on the Syracuse basketball game that blared from the television and played on—even after I barked at him to turn the volume down. Feeling sorry for myself, I curled inward where I could sink into a meditation on reality and time and my own aging because "'men don't turn to look at me anymore'" either.

If I had actually said these words, my voice would have been like Chantal's, "bitter and melancholy," as I resigned to fate and fact. Time diminishes a woman's capacity to cause sparks in the gender rub, diminishes the urgency of her feminine presence, diminishes her power. Something that I had never used every day, but enjoyed when I did, has gone missing. As if the sturdy ceramic mugs stand waiting in the cupboard, but the china teacup with its rippled gold rim and scattered wild violets has vanished. As if the bulky heaps of cotton underwear huddle in the dresser drawer, ready for duty, but the froth of mauve lace has disappeared from the back corner, leaving only the faintest ginger scent from its veil of sighs and whispers. I did not notice a moment or a day in my life when it happened, but the allure exuded by youth and presumed fertility has evanesced and I, like Chantal, have begun a public disappearance. Kundera's musings and speculations about the target of his fictional gaze insinuated a shadowy lacking into my own consciousness, and I found myself drifting between now and then.

———

Chantal checks into a hotel on the Normandy coast, alone until her live-in lover, Jean-Marc, can join her the next day. Dreams harrow her sleep and she finds that "the past came lumbering in," bringing with it her ex-husband, his new wife, and various yesteryear seductions. When she rises, she leaves the room to walk on the beach—only to find fathers with "meek, solicitous" expressions planted amidst family chaos: "She imagines trying to flirt with a daddy pushing a stroller with one baby inside it and carrying another two babies on his back and belly." Fixated on the drought of lusty looks coming her way, Chantal attempts to blame her audience, "men have daddified themselves," but cannot still her desire for the sexual tension caused by men noticing her as they once did.

When Jean-Marc and Chantal later meet in the hotel room, she seems sad and does not look like herself. Pressed for an explanation she admits, "'Men don't turn to look at me anymore.'" Then she feels Jean-Marc studying her, and "deep inside her body that gaze was touching off a fire." Flushed and "burning like a torch," Chantal feels ashamed and misunderstood as she realizes that now, because the currents in her body betray her without warning, Jean-Marc might believe he knows her "secret yearnings."

At first, Jean-Marc feels inadequate when Chantal bemoans her fading power to attract the male gaze. Isn't his attention enough? But he moves past implications which diminish him as a partner, and instead seizes upon the swerving nature of the feminine journey through time, suspecting that "every woman measures how much she's aged by the interest or uninterest men show in her body." He concludes that it is impossible for him to satisfy what Chantal finds lacking: "No, what she needs is not a loving gaze but a flood of alien, crude, lustful looks settling on her. . . . Those are the looks that sustain her within human society. The gaze of love rips her out of it."

———

Up and down the streets of a university ghetto during the late 1970s and early 80s, young families teeming with boisterous children filled most of the starter houses that cost nearly more than any of us could afford. Unless school or stormy weather interfered, the sidewalks churned with Big Wheels powered by reckless boys pumping the pedals hard and fast, all the way to enough. Little girls pranced back and forth in their mothers' old taffeta prom dresses, teetering on too-large high heels as they ignored the rambunctious riders. During a lull in activity on one such day, the plaintive voice of my seven-year-old son asked an eight-year-old girl if she wanted to play at his house, and she snubbed him with a flip of her tangled red hair. She said that she was going to Megan's and hurried past him, still clearly preferring to be with—and be admired by—her own sex.

Predictable events set life's rhythm back then. Most fathers left early and returned late, walking the few blocks to their work on campus or at the medical center. Stay-at-home mothers managed varying degrees of commitment to housework, wandered outdoors to watch over children, talked to each other between pursuits of runaways, and talked to each other in pursuit of sanity. Sometimes before I'd even cooked breakfast, the Mormon family across the street had released four boys between the ages of two and nine into the neighborhood, all raring to play but still more eager to enter a house where a forbidden television squawked out cartoons. A young mother from up the street could often be spotted on the sidewalk wearing her bathrobe while she pulled a child-filled wagon, hovered behind various plastic vehicles, or simply walked a restless toddler. My widowed neighbor, who believed she had raised a son to adult perfection, puttered in her yard, ready to notice and later comment on the latest proof of inept parenting and kids gone wild.

And then around mid-afternoon, a recently divorced friend might wander up the street to sit on my front stoop and replay scenes from her life. Her former husband, a surgical resident at the hospital, had announced on Father's Day a couple years before that he was leaving her and their two toddlers for another woman. I heard details about young love and great sex as she retraced the domestic path that had taken her over a cliff. She wanted to explain to a sympathetic listener—and to herself—why she had married someone who was so emotionally distant, someone who didn't love her anymore. Discussion inevitably turned into trash-talk about her cheating ex-husband, and then drifted into ways that she might stretch the child support money and fill her loneliness.

Pride eventually rose to displace some of my friend's grief and she focused her energy on making he-who-had-gone look like a fool to have left. Pregnancies might have packed pounds onto her frame, but she would show him. She was ready to revamp her Swedish good looks with the mean magic of diet and weight lifting. So the dreary months of an upstate New York winter passed with updates on how a newly single woman prepares for a return to the dating game. Then, when warm weather returned, my friend stripped down in her backyard and soaked up the sun while the kids played in the sandbox. On a trip to a local discount chain, she bought a khaki tube dress that fit like a second skin to wear with new wedge-heeled sandals that were tan-colored, to make her legs look longer. The effect of her sun-bleached hair, taut, glistening flesh, and optimistic attitude came down to one thing: This woman was hot.

Ordinary life paused one sweltry day for the annual neighborhood picnic. On a Saturday afternoon, sawhorses blocked off traffic, lawn mowers stopped, and doors flew open so we could all spill into the street. Adults carried bowls and platters to the card tables that had been arranged across a section of the road, and children shot off in search of their own kind like an assortment of heat-seeking devices. Tuna macaroni salads, bean casseroles, and overbaked bundt cakes seemed to multiply, and recipes became the topic of the day for thickening women in Bermuda shorts who clustered around relish trays. Posturing men, who seldom talked to each other around the neighborhood, joked and had a few beers while watching the sizzle of hamburgers and hot dogs on kettle-shaped grills. The mother-women glanced over to gauge the picnic spirits of husbands, and did periodic head counts of children who chalked, hop-scotched, and raced on the suddenly safe road. But then our no-longer-married neighbor, wearing her new dress, rounded the corner at the stop sign and started a hip-roll up the main drag.

Perhaps the strappy sandals made her walk like that while carrying a dish to pass, or she might have been powered by sheer determination, but with breasts bobbling under insufficient khaki, she brought carnal possibility into the light of day and rattled more than one family romance. Laughing and swaying, she parted the throngs of unleashed dogs and crazed bikers as she tossed her pale, shimmering hair for what seemed like miles. Everyone older than twelve pretended not to be spellbound, pretended not to hear *ba-boom, ba-boom* pulsing through the heavy air, pretended to look at something other than this sexy woman devouring the runway until they could resist no longer and just had to let their eyes touch her one more time. Her own children poked at each other from their rear flank positions during this drama, and finally my own husband broke the fat dumbness of us all when he muttered, "Hi, Max," to her son, even though he scarcely noticed the physical child whom he addressed.

Why do I see my blonde friend's effect on us that day so clearly, so enviously? I still secretly wish that I had been looked at in that way, but I wasn't. Instead, from those same years, I recall a cocky voice from a speeding car full of teenaged boys yelling, "Hey, Mama!" as I jogged near the street where I'd once seen a village virtually hypnotized. Perhaps memory exaggerates my friend's sexual power because I'm now fixated on my own loss of looks, because I'm trying to understand precisely what it is that I must do without. Or perhaps I confuse literature with life, as sometimes happens, and my thoughts fumble through images until I create a sham rendition of Shakespeare's Cleopatra enthroned on her barge. Amidst a perfumed cloud, the eternal temptress calls forth an entire city and causes Enobarbus to proclaim: "Age cannot wither her, nor custom stale / Her infinite variety." Milan Kundera sees Chantal (and women like me) wishing for that feminine glory to settle over us and go on and on.

———

"'I follow you around like a spy—you are beautiful, very beautiful.'" An anonymous admirer writes to Chantal and describes gazing at her, desiring her. She means to destroy the letters, but hesitates because they excite her; instead, she hides them in a drawer among her brassieres which "suddenly looked vulgar and idiotically feminine." Simply knowing that the letters exist awakens her sensuality and she becomes keenly aware of her body while watching for her watcher. As the letters that follow become more erotic, their images fuel Chantal's own fantasies and she begins to participate in the text. Her admirer writes: "'Thinking of you, I fling a mantle stitched of flame over your naked body. I swathe your white body in a cardinal's crimson mantle. And then I put you, draped like that, into a red room on a red bed, my red cardinal, most gorgeous cardinal!'" So Chantal buys a red nightgown to see herself through a phantom lover's eyes, to become the woman of his imagination. Veiled in scarlet, she surprises Jean-Marc with a game of seduction in which they are both "intoxicated by the image of a woman running from a man who desires her."

The passion generated by knowledge of being watched and admired shatters the boredom that had crept into Chantal's life. Yet *needing* the letters causes her to feel guilt and embarrassment, and dictates that they remain hidden. Attempting to solve the mystery of her anonymous suitor, Chantal speculates about a young man who is a regular customer at the neighborhood bistro, and then about the beggar who leans against a tree outside her apartment. She imagines scenes in which each man is enamored with her, but later feels pathetic when evidence indicates that neither man is her special admirer: "Why is she paying so much attention to this bullshit?" Is she a "romantic and stupid woman," so desperate to be noticed that she clings to a stranger's fantasies?

Early one New Year's Eve morning, I gripped a cane to limp across a slush-covered supermarket parking lot on my recently broken left foot. A forty-year-old woman wearing a frayed wool coat, baggy pants, and a temporary cast: I was a mess. But this errand could be accomplished with unbrushed teeth and unbrushed hair; the goal was to purchase food and return home before my children were awake. I tossed the cane into a grocery cart, adjusted my purse, and launched a halting advance through the aisles. Bread, soup, tuna, paper towels, tissues, detergent. Then it happened in produce, by the potatoes: "You sure ain't gonna be doin' much dancin' tonight," crooned a low, manly voice.

What? I looked up to meet the eager eyes of a man with slicked back brown hair, the kind that holds rigid, oily comb tracks. He nodded toward my cast, as if to explain his comment, and I tried to process our interaction while taking in the sheen of his turquoise satin jacket. My befuddled reply was, "No, I guess not."

He forged ahead: "What you need is a big feller who could pick you right up."

With an awkward smile that was little more than a reflex, I stammered, "I guess so," before trudging past cooking onions and winter squash. Surprised by the attention of an apparent admirer, but disappointed by how unattractive he was, my response lacked anything that could be interpreted as enthusiasm. Even so, I could not resist a backward glance at my smooth-talker. White embroidered script arched across the back of his glossy jacket to introduce "Duane," and I have not forgotten.

———

After finding Chantal's hidden letters, Jean-Marc becomes jealous and resents that she guards a private fantasy life—even though he knows that she has not been unfaithful. Memory, imagination, and reality become entangled, one nearly inextricable from another; suspicion and doubt quietly undermine their relationship as each partner interrogates the identity of self and other. But through a lens of tenderness, Jean-Marc sees that Chantal embodies "his sole emotional link to the world," and realizes that, in theory, he wants her to experience the pleasure of being admired, of feeling "captivated." Reminding himself that life presents "[t]he tree of possibilities" with its "canopy filled with bees singing," he concludes that he wants Chantal to "hear the music of a murmuring treetop" in reality—because he loves her.

Then the last secret letter arrives to inform Chantal that her mysterious admirer must leave: "'Is this departure really unexpected or, rather, did I not write these letters precisely because I knew they would have no aftermath? Wasn't it the certainty of my departure that allowed me to speak to you with utter candor?'"

———

Perhaps the last time was in Bethesda. My daughter and I were meeting her college roommate at the subway stop before joining the rest of our family for dinner at a Mongolian restaurant down the block. While my impatient girl paced and searched inside the station, I waited outside at the street level exit where an escalator delivered passengers into the honey glow of a summer evening.

People everywhere. The view over the railing—down into the station, into the waves of workers and wanderers as they stepped off one bank of escalators and onto the next—shifted constantly in a tableau of urban entropy. Watching the nameless negotiate escape from the underworld, I possessed what they sought: I was drenched in the day's last sunshine. Each corrugated stair kept rising, rising—mechanical Sisyphus rolling riders toward me until they shared my ground—then slipped back down into the darkness to begin again with new passengers. I tried to cut individuals from the collage of heads that sliced around and through each other, looking for a young woman with quick eyes and curly hair. Searching, searching, only to be distracted by one, then another, and another who were not the one.

Their lives were easy to imagine and they filled my idleness. An hour ago, the scuffed brown wing tips that stepped off beside me had moved with false steadiness through a corporate office where downsizing had been announced. Now their hunched occupant shuffled toward the corner bar, toward the despair of tomorrow. The woman with smudged eye make-up, the one wearing a snug, white silk blouse, hoped to hurry home to shower away evidence of infidelity. The red linen dress that stood out in the crowd had hung on a hook in a curtained cubicle earlier in the day. Its occupant, who was around my age, seemed stalwart and would not weep until she reached home. But still no dinner guest. Was there another exit from the station? Had I, the street lookout, botched my job?

Then a tall man wearing a suit and carrying a leather briefcase joined the ascending escalator crowd. To be honest, I was attracted to his story because he was strikingly handsome. The subtle pin stripe of his light wool suit, the sharp edges of trimmed brown hair with moments of gray, and the droop of his shoulders as he stared down at nothing promised money and sadness. I stared at his emptiness while possibilities danced through my head. There had been a terrible disappointment in his life. A death? No, perhaps a betrayal or a shattering failure gnawed at his heart. Then he looked up and caught me watching. I glanced away with practiced nonchalance. But the escalator, unlikely to change course, carried him steadily closer. Feigning interest in other targets, I waltzed away his loneliness as I replayed the meeting of our eyes, pulsing the time it would take him to reach street level. The escalator kept cranking upward and as he neared my woozy height, our eyes met again and he asked, "I don't suppose you're waiting for me, are you?"

Not so secretly delighted, I answered, "I'm waiting for a nineteen-year-old girl with curly hair." Having regained solid ground, he paused and smiled before merging into the anonymous crowd that hurried away from me. Our encounter was over, with "no aftermath."

Yet I was changed. Just as I had created stories about each of those travelers whom I culled from the crowd, I began to imagine myself beautiful, with glints of gold sparkling through my red hair, and the tiniest lines laughing near my lips. *Over and over again, a tall man touches his hand to the nape of my neck, nestling his fingers into my hair. He inhales the azure of my eyes, the dark blueness of my summer dress, and then brushing his lips beneath my ear he whispers, "I don't suppose you're waiting for me, are you?"*

The Last Good Obsession

Jean-Marc and Chantal argue after a visit from her ex-sister-in-law: He sees an "unfamiliar" Chantal who "is not the woman he loves," and she sees a man who spies on her and fails to respect her privacy. After shutting herself in her room, she sleeps fitfully amidst dreams that are erotic and disturbing: "Each time she wakes after such dreams, she feels uneasy. That, she thinks, is one of the secrets of a woman's life, every woman's: the nocturnal promiscuity that renders suspect all promises of fidelity, all purity, all innocence." Chantal savors the notion of long ago virgins and saints imagining themselves engaged in debauchery, and she pictures "Mother Teresa running in a sweat through the world, doing her good works" after nights of dreaming "unacknowledgeable, improbable, imbecilic vices."

———————

I lie on a narrow bed. The room around me feels damp and cold and I don't want to get up. I reach for a heavy black shawl that drapes across the chair by the desk and wrap its thick folds around my shoulders. Alone and lonely in a Paris hotel, I can't seem to get warm; I phone for coffee to be sent to my room and wait, huddled beneath the covers until there's a knock on the door. I get up and open the door to see a young woman holding a tray that I take in exchange for a large coin. Alone again, I pour steaming coffee into a white cup and stand at the window taking sips, looking at the street below, occasionally glancing down at the laptop and jumbled papers that cover the desk. Stories that refuse to be written.

I study my face in the mirror and begin smoothing make-up across my skin. Turning the compact that contains cheek blush, I see that the color is called Hopeful; uncapping the eyeliner pencil, gold letters along the shaft inform me that Dusk will encircle my eyes. My public face complete, I dress with care, layering lacy underwear, black stockings, gray tweed skirt, red cashmere sweater, and the wool shawl. I pin my hair in a twist, slip into black shoes, grab my purse, and leave the room, hurrying through the hall toward steep stairs that lead down to a dark foyer with a heavy glass door. But when I step onto the sidewalk, I feel confused and don't know where I should go.

I finally turn toward a tree with heart-shaped leaves, but I walk slowly, trying not to step on pavement cracks. A café sign—Le Chat Rouge—becomes visible beyond the tree and when I reach it, I open a door that causes a bell to jingle. After asking a woman behind a counter for a croissant and coffee, I carry my food to a table near the front windows and sit down to eat and read until I know what happens next.

The book I remove from my purse is Milan Kundera's *Identity*; I press it open and try to smooth the final pages. *I will think about men and women, love and lust, and of course—identity. Let's say a woman craves the touch of a man's desiring gaze—to feel more alive. Does she lose identity by dancing the dance meant to win the attention of a potential admirer? Is she more or less alive for having adapted her own self to another's fantasies? Think: If she chooses to reveal her "secret yearnings," does she ever after feel observed, "in a cage like a rabbit"? Does she?*

But reading on, I find that Chantal's challenges are not quite as I'd imagined, and I smack the book closed, suspicious that Kundera choreographed an erotic game to string me along while he explores reality and fantasy. I want to remain with Chantal, struggling with vanity and desire and fidelity; I don't want the spell of a lovers' tale broken by authorial intrusion: "Who dreamed this story? Who imagined it? She? He? Both of them? Each one for the other? And starting when did their real life change into this treacherous fantasy?" *Dreamed? The repercussions of doubt that Chantal and Jean-Marc suffer might be part of a dream? She didn't leave after an argument, expecting him to move out of her apartment? There was no reason for me to worry about her safety when she's cold and naked at a London orgy? They're really together, at home, tucked in bed, safe and sound? Whose sentimental, happily-ever-after dream is that?*

Just then, a man with short, silvery hair stops next to my table and says, "I've watched you reading. You look very beautiful in your red sweater, like a schoolgirl with her book. Do you like this book?"

"Thank you, and, yes, I like it very much—even though the ending has caused me to feel confused. Have you read it?" But none of that comes out smoothly; I'm blushing and stumbling over words that refuse to cooperate.

"You might say I know the story. I am Milan Kundera."

"Oh, I see—now I see." *I'd imagined him taller, younger, but still, he's very attractive. Please, please don't let me gush "I love your books," or worse yet, "I love your looks."*

"Each morning I walk past this café, but today, I stopped because I saw you through the window, reading very closely, underlining, taking notes in the margins. A naughty schoolgirl skipping class to be alone."

I look into the dark eyes that pierce my own dusky ones and turn up the heat of a carefully calibrated smile. Holding his gaze until it drops to my quivering breasts, I begin to feel hopeful and press ahead: "How does their story really end? I feel happy believing that Jean-Marc actually writes the letters to Chantal, thinking himself a sort of Cyrano. That part is still true, isn't it? And I can't accept this ending. You can't mean that the guilt, the shame, the anger are only part of a dream? Those things are *real.* I don't want to be guessing about the borders of reality and fantasy. I want to know."

"Forget them. Come with me for a walk in the Luxembourg Gardens." He takes my hand and raises me from the chair, pulling me toward him as if he knows my secret yearnings. "I want to show you someone. I visit her each day where she waits for me in the garden, a statue. I call her my Hélène and you remind me of her—but alive." He nudges me toward the door, his hand igniting a blaze as it slides the length of my back.

—

A few months after my husband and I returned from our vacation in Savannah, I was hired to teach composition at a local community college. I shared an office with eight other instructors who either didn't want or couldn't get full-time employment. There, in those close quarters, I learned that serving as adjunct faculty holds no glamour. But I liked some of the people I worked with, and they helped me survive the mind-numbing experience of reading and grading seventy informative essays—only to face seventy persuasive essays a few weeks later.

Of the group wedged into the room we sometimes called the "kennel," I was the oldest at fifty-five, followed by a woman named Toni who hovered somewhere in her mid-forties. The men sharing that space were significantly younger, but Toni joked with each of them about being his girlfriend, or, in mock devotion, his fiancée. Her Brooklyn smart-talk had us all laughing, whether she was confronting a student about the difference between truth and lies—"Don't fuck with me!"—or trying to convince us to go out for drinks. We watched her interpretation of womanhood with affectionate admiration, a rapt audience while she pushed back her tumbling black hair, lifted an eyebrow to frame the mischief in her eyes, or shaped a Chanel red pout. She filled our stark, cinderblock headquarters with buzzing energy.

One afternoon I stood sorting my mail beside a fake veneer desk, tired and nearly ready to go home, while Chris and Keith talked quietly in front of a computer screen. Then Toni came sweeping through the doorway looking particularly sexy, and announced her breezy good mood: "Hi, guys."

"Toni! You look really beautiful today," I gushed, feeling suddenly more energetic. "You've got the hair working, the make-up is just right, the sweater, the pearls, everything." And I meant it; she looked beautiful.

With that, she moved closer to me and put her arm around my shoulder. "Well, thank you, but it would be nice if Chris or Keith had said that. They don't pay any attention to me."

Both men stared, momentarily speechless, while Toni and I stood waiting, each with an arm resting on the other's shoulder. Chris, twenty-six and known to complain that women aren't sufficiently interested in him, tried to meet her challenge. Gazing at the two women who were each old enough to be his mother, he announced: "Toni, you always look beautiful. And Sandra, you look . . . smart."

Noticing the pause while he searched for an adjective, I chose to rationalize that my heavy black-rimmed glasses (think Buddy Holly) must have determined his eventual choice: Smart. I laughed and told him, "Thanks a lot," but I wanted smart *and* beautiful.

———

Each time I tell the story of looking "smart," I turn my disappointment into a joke. And then, when I'm alone, I sometimes think of Chantal. Somehow, she leads me to a hazy place where my own guarded secrets creep from dark corners, where I remember or imagine the tingle of a gaze skimming over my body, and the pleasure of sometimes glancing back. Confusion about what is mine and what is Chantal's has caused me to re-read her story more than once, because there's more to her life—to my life—than suggested on the surface.

Chantal once "wanted to be a rose fragrance, a pervasive, overwhelming fragrance, she wanted to move thus through all men and, by way of the men, to embrace the entire world." But I've come to think that Kundera does not mean for Chantal to simply wither, a time-sensitive bloom in a vast, impersonal garden. Amidst her worries about public disappearance, he nudges her into searching beyond her physical, sexual substance, into remembering scenes from a failed marriage, the death of her five-year-old son, and the considerable evidence of her own will to succeed and survive. Chantal finds precious clues to her own nature and to the mysteries of life and love while indulging her imaginative life—and in spite of having hot flashes.

Re-reading *Identity* opened an ending that I first perceived as making a too tidy bed in which the lovers only have eyes for each other. Jean-Marc wakes Chantal after he hears her cry out in her sleep, and holds her, assuring her that the dream she experienced isn't "'real.'" Kundera interrupts the lovers' embrace (an apparent case of authorial prerogative) and suggests that the convoluted trials of ego and intimacy, slipping further and further back in time, might be nothing more than Chantal's imagination at work; their relationship is really fine. That's when I silently accused him of trying to diminish the challenges in feminine experience.

Yet on the last page, Kundera leaves the bedroom light switched on so that Chantal can look at Jean-Marc as they lie next to each other. Rather than settle for the sappy, happily-ever-after interpretation of my first reading, I now suspect that Kundera wants to show me that love can and must endure scrutiny if it is to survive. In questioning reality and fantasy for his fictional couple, Kundera nudges me to understand that those boundaries *cannot* be neatly drawn; being alive is frustrating and thrilling business, if done right. So I wonder: When *isn't* my life whirling in a cloud of reality and fantasy? When am I *not* sorting through the seductive buzz of possibilities—some touchable, some thinkable—that fill my days and nights? When am I *not* secretly hoping for an admiring look? But then, after remembering the scent of roses or ginger, after imagining fingers that unfasten my hair or slide down my spine, I see that I swim against the currents that mean to divert me and return to the bed where I am loved best.

Living with Goodness

Sometimes in the night Charles woke up with a start, thinking he
was being called to a patient: "I'm coming," he stammered.
—Gustave Flaubert, *Madame Bovary*

The first ring at 4:37 a.m. shatters the dark, hitting like a heart
attack and jolting me awake into confused panic. *What happened? Who?* Sometimes I'm sitting bolt upright before the second ring,
and usually my husband has successfully groped beneath last night's
books and magazines to grab the phone before the third. One side of
the conversation is all I ever hear, all I really need to hear:

"How much blood?"

"Where's it coming from?"

"Okay, but is it coming out his nose, his mouth, his trach?"

"It always looks like a lot, but how much do you think?"

"What's his INR?"

"You need a surgeon to look at him. Who's there?"

"ENT? What do they say?"

"Get a chest X-ray. I'll come in. Maybe a bronchoscope will show
something."

—

Sometimes at night when I cannot quiet my mind and drift off to
sleep, I make my joke about pulmonary medicine being boring, not

glamorous like cardiology or surgery. "Put me to sleep; talk to me about sputum," I say to my husband. But that's just one little piece of the story. Another piece is that after thirty-four years of sharing a bed with a lung specialist who gets consultation calls during hoped-for sleep, the startle effect of that phone jangle has not softened. Fear that something has happened to one of our kids or my widowed mother predictably triggers whole-body response: My chest hammers and my head bangs until time reveals that the portion of grief currently being dispensed belongs to someone else.

During this particular blood-stained morning, the phone clunking back into its socket signals my chance to say what I always say: "What happened?" The least I can do is ask and listen, but mostly I let my body slacken and sag into the warm sheets with utter relief.

"It's crazy. Sounds like this guy's hemorrhaging from his lungs. He's in the ER and nobody can figure out what's causing it."

"Yikes," I mumble.

"This is the father of the disabled kid with the weird genetic syndrome and a lot of lung troubles. The kid's actually doing okay at the moment."

"Mmm, I remember. . ."—but by then I'm drifting off.

———

In *Madame Bovary*, the mistress of the house does not waken to a phone ringing, but to someone rapping on the door and calling her husband's name. Being a nineteenth-century doctor in rural France, Charles Bovary maintains an office in his home, where "in the kitchen one could hear the people coughing in the consulting-room and recounting their whole histories." But Emma Bovary shows little interest in their stories; she's consumed by her own. Driven by narcissism and endless wanting, she longs "to find out what one meant exactly in life by the words *bliss, passion, ecstasy,* that had seemed to her so beautiful in books." Emma aspires to romantic manifestations of happiness when she marries the "saviour" who treated her father's broken leg, but her fantasies of wifehood fail to materialize. Instead, she finds herself living an ordinary life with an ordinary man who tends the sick—but "could neither swim, nor fence, nor shoot, and one day he could not explain some term of horsemanship to her that she had come across in a novel." Emma Bovary finds the faithful doctor and his steadfast ways to be boring:

> He came home late—at ten o'clock, at midnight sometimes. Then he asked for something to eat, and as the servant had gone to bed, Emma waited on him. He took off his coat to dine more at his ease. He told her, one after the other, the people he had met, the villages where he had been, the prescriptions he had written, and well pleased with himself, he finished the remainder of the boiled beef, peeled the crust of his cheese, munched an apple, finished the wine, and then went to bed, lay on his back and snored.

And then she circles her discontent until she targets the heart of the matter: "Why, for heaven's sake, did I marry?"

———

It must be love of humanity that keeps my husband going. As a physician who cares for patients, instructs medical students, and oversees medical residents at a teaching hospital, he is required to record his work hours for one week during each quarter to assure that the institution receives Medicare reimbursement. Sitting at his desk in our bedroom one night, he seemed ingenuous while reporting that he had worked seventy-two hours the previous week: "I thought it had been a pretty light week until I saw the numbers and actually thought about it." When I pressed him on the subject, he admitted that the worst weekly tallies are in the nineties and the lightest in the fifties. There I was with nothing more demanding to do than read in bed, so I launched my usual rant about the hospital's abuse of full-time faculty. I blustered that the administration will never provide additional salary support to hire new doctors as long as people like him are willing to work themselves to death. But my passive-aggressive nature knows full well that caring for patients really matters to him, he *cares* about their lives and life stories. So, after a few volleys, I eased up and let him end the conversation: "It's not bad unless I'm in the ICU. Besides, lots of people work hard."

———

Some jobs are harder than they seem at first glance: "I will prescribe regimens for the good of my patients according to my ability and my judgment and never do harm to anyone" (a familiar summation of Hippocratic ethical code, c. 400 BCE).

———

After Emma experiences the seduction of glamour during a weekend at a wealthy patient's estate, her desire for "something to happen" only intensifies; her heart is changed forever, as if "something had rubbed off on it that could not be removed." The delectable Emma studies magazines to keep up with society events and the latest styles, and reads Balzac and George Sand hoping to find "imaginary satisfaction for her own desires." Feeling stuck in what seemed "the mediocrity of existence," she assumes more affectations to color her drab world, costuming herself with attention to detail—gold buttons, tassels, and "small wine-red slippers" with a "large knot of ribbon that fell over her instep." Looking ever-so-beautiful, she plots to insinuate her-self amidst the privileged: She buys proper writing supplies, studies herself in the mirror, reads dreamily, and imagines traveling, all the while confusing "the sensuous pleasures of luxury with the delights of the heart, elegance of manners with delicacy of sentiment." Bored, self-absorbed, and trapped, Emma "wanted to die, but she also wanted to live in Paris."

Meanwhile, Charles makes house calls through inclement weather to relieve suffering. He "poked his arm into damp beds, received the tepid spurt of blood-letting in his face, listened to death-rattles, examined basins, turned over a good deal of dirty linen." Having established a reputation for being "specially successful with heavy colds and chest ailments," and having proved that he "was not proud," many people love and admire him. After long days and nights of sobering work, Charles returns to an irresistible, restless wife who plays an imagined role to sustain herself. Her loveliness, the scent of her perfume, and the refinements with which she surrounds herself conjure a mysterious world that captivates Charles, lifting him from the mundane as if by enchantment: "It was like a golden dust sanding all along the narrow path of his life."

***

During the two years that we were together in Syracuse, New York, my husband was immersed in an internal medicine residency—a sophisticated, low-paying apprenticeship—while I finished a degree in nursing and worked in a hospital. Then I tagged along to Columbus, Ohio for his two years of service with the U.S. Air Force (payback for not being taken by the draft during the middle stages of the Vietnam War). Military work hours were relatively short, the patients were generally healthy, we had more money than ever before, and base housing provided a ready supply of other young couples who liked to socialize. We played tennis, discovered new restaurants nearly each week, and traveled to Europe and the Caribbean. It was frivolous fun, a life that a twentieth-century Emma Bovary might enjoy.

When the time came to leave, I was eight months pregnant with the baby I had been longing for, and my bulging middle could no longer fit safely behind the steering wheel of my 1970 Triumph Spitfire convertible. We sold my dream car to scrape up a down payment on a $32,000 pink aluminum-sided house in Rochester, New York, near the hospital where a delivery room awaited me and a two-year pulmonary fellowship awaited my husband.

———

The arrival of a baby girl, rather than the son who might have provided "revenge for all her impotence in the past," further complicates Emma's disappointment with life; for her, flirting with "gentlemen" is far preferable to caring for a child or a husband or a home. When she hears of a scheme by which Charles could gain fame and fortune as a doctor specializing in clubfoot repair, she imagines the reflection of his glory providing her with something better than love. Hoping to please her, hoping for success, Charles studies a description of the procedure, performs it on a stable worker, and causes real harm. Suffering gangrene and intractable pain, the patient requires attention from an experienced surgeon who finds it necessary to amputate the leg. Humiliation hangs over the Bovary house as naïveté verging on stupidity fuels Charles' reasoning about what went wrong. All the while, Emma fills with rage over her perceived sacrifices, and she finds revenge and pleasure in buying luxuries—such as "a riding-crop with its silver-gilt top" for her not-so-secret lover, and "a large lined cloak with a deep collar" for herself—while she plans her escape to a romantic life.

———

Pretty things whisper of elusive pleasures. Hungry for adult interactions, restless to escape the tight walls of our little house, I buckled baby into his car seat and headed for the closest suburban mall in our Volkswagen Dasher station wagon. He didn't seem to mind viewing the world of knees from his stroller while I tried to satisfy my craving to touch lace lingerie, silky dresses, velvet hats, and Italian leather shoes. Not that I could afford to buy any of those things; I was unemployed and my husband was being paid a small stipend by the university hospital where he saw patients and worked on research. Besides, my clothes were under constant threat of spit-up and diaper leaks.

One fall afternoon, the two of us were browsing through a nice department store and I was drawn to the glove counter, perhaps because I was coming to grips with the fact that pregnancy had altered everything about my shape but hand size. Gazing into a glass case to admire a pair made of dark russet-colored wool, I told the saleslady, who had shown little interest in me, that I'd like a closer look at them. But a quick scan of baby and me and our sensible clothes was all she needed; she managed a stiff smile while stating, "They're cashmere," but made no move to take them out for my inspection. I assumed that she had made a judgment about my ability to pay for them.

With that, I had to have them. "Yes, they look lovely. Please bring them out." Reluctantly, she removed them from protective custody and placed them on the counter. I lifted one so I might wiggle my chapped fingers into the lush knit, and then held my hand up to admire the perfect glove. Without asking the price, I gave each fingertip a casual tug, returned the glove to its mate, and said, "I'll take them." Silenced, as I had intended her to be, she went to the cash register while I dug into my purse for the credit card that would allow me to walk out of the store carrying cashmere. Next day, baby and I went to a branch store at a different mall where I returned my purchase, explaining to a *nice* saleslady that I'd changed my mind. With $42 credited to my account, I hustled us out of there before other temptations could lure me.

Charles Bovary and his optimistic yet idiotic attempt at clubfoot repair would be a present-day insurance company's nightmare. But litigious society had not yet evolved, so the damaged patient murmurs nothing of malpractice claims, and overall he causes little trouble about the mutilation of his body. Charles buys him an intricate wooden leg complete with cork covering, spring-loaded joints, and "ending in a patent-leather boot"; and when that proves impractical for daily wear, he also pays for a plainer model. Eventually "the tap of the wooden leg on pavement" is heard through the village as the young victim attempts to negotiate daily life. But Emma shows little concern for her role in the disaster, proving herself beyond recovery of any tolerance for Charles. She is consumed with desire to escape a life that she now finds unbearable.

———

I listen. I watch. I'm behind the scenes, a witness to crises of living and dying faced by real people whose names are rightly unknown to me—unless they tell me as part of a phone message for my husband. On occasion, I've been pulled into the spectacle when one thing or another tips precariously off balance.

Dizzying advances in medical technology and pharmaceuticals allow modern health care consumers to expect that nearly everyone can be saved. Sometimes in the most hopeless cases, families demand everything possible be done to prolong life until a miracle arrives. If a patient has not left a prior directive about limits on treatment, family members may find it unbearable to let go. My husband not infrequently consults on patients who are comatose and without reasonable chance of recovery, and in one particular case, a patient's family threatened legal action if every possible life-sustaining measure was not administered. So day after day, a ventilator pumped oxygen into a body that had shut down. Nurses continued to wash and turn the patient whose skin sloughed off under their touch—and they often left the room in tears. One morning before light, our phone rang to report the man's death. On hearing this news, my husband spoke of mercy, and afterwards wondered aloud if the unrelenting family would sue over his failure to divine a cure.

During a rotation of ICU work, an HIV/AIDS patient spiraled toward death under my husband's care, but, in compliance with the patient's wishes, the family could not be told the diagnosis. Dozens of relatives hovered at the bedside, unable to comprehend why their loved one was so ill, why he was not recovering. Their grief and rage accumulated over several days until the nearness of death caused them to erupt in accusations against the only outsider in the room, the good doctor. Shouting about incompetence and insinuating physical threats, they frightened the nurses, who called for security guards. They wanted *that* doctor barred from the room. They wanted the patient moved to a different hospital that would provide adequate care. And my husband still could not tell them why their son, their brother, their nephew, their cousin continued to die after everything possible had been done to save him.

When he returned home that night, my husband looked beaten while recounting the emotional toll of the day: How to process the family's threats, the guards standing in the hall out of concern for his safety, and his own sustained silence to honor the patient's wishes? The dying man's friend and confidant had thanked him for his care and apologized for the family's behavior, words that brought comfort in the wake of having felt a little afraid. On finishing his account, my husband said, "Keep the doors locked, just in case. A couple people in the family were acting really crazy and I guess it's possible that they might try to do something." For a few weeks, our doors were bolted.

———

How do I roll over and complain about having a morning headache to someone who's dressing for work in the predawn darkness? How do I explain that I don't want to get up and grade composition papers because they're even worse than the terrible ones of last semester? How do I mention, as if in passing, that I feel sad when I waken? Sometimes I whine, "My head's killing me. Would you bring me a couple Advil and a cup of coffee?" *That's right, headache before asthma, apnea, pneumonia, and even respiratory failure.* Still other times, I don't bother to pretend that I'd get up at that very moment if only I felt better; I stay curled in a heap feeling sorry for myself while he finishes his morning rituals, while he's on the expressway, while he's sequestered with another family that wants to know if death will soon come calling.

Prevented by her sex from living boldly, yet using her sex to chase after evanescent dreams, Emma Bovary careens toward ruin. To support her taste for luxury, she steals from her husband's accounts, repeatedly borrows money from a local loan shark, and sinks to pawning silver spoons given to her as a wedding gift by her father. Discarded by one lover, embraced by another, Emma engages with life as if performing scenes in which she might reinvent herself. She even uses a façade of goodness to win over her next ardent admirer when she proposes, "'What I would like . . . is to work in a hospital as a nursing Sister.'" Once more entangled in her search for bliss, Emma once more finds that adultery, like marriage, is flawed, and her "irritable, greedy, voluptuous" nature resurfaces.

A court order to seize all Bovary property for nonpayment of debts sets the final stage for Emma's undoing. She knows that Charles will go on blindly loving her, as he has in the past: "'Yes,' she murmured, grinding her teeth, 'he will forgive me, the man I could never forgive for having known me. . . .'" His "magnanimity exasperated her," and there would be no escaping "the weight of his generosity." So, after exhausting other solutions, she eats arsenic to end her life; "she was through with lying, cheating, and with the numberless desires that had tortured her." Dying, she tells her husband, "'you're good, not like the others,'" and shows more love for him and their child than ever she did in life. The effects of the poison cause her to vomit blood and scream in agony until "the spectacle of Emma dying" is over.

———

Living with goodness says, "Hush." Yet there are times I feel like screaming and one day I painted our kitchen the red of watery blood. Ripe tomatoes from our garden were piled in an eight-quart basket, waiting for me to transform them into marinara sauce as I'd promised, but I was alone and the house was still, and I began throwing them. And I was alone afterwards while I washed the walls and floors and cupboards.

———

Sometimes when I press *Play* on the answering machine, voices belonging to worried strangers are waiting, though not for me: "Hi, Doctor. This is Louise and, ah, ah, Arnie seems to be having a reaction to the medication and I wanted to see if you could help me. I'd appreciate your call. Thank you. Bye. Oh, my number is. . . ."

She sounds old and frail; she sounds nice, *means* to sound nice hoping that the niceness will expedite the return call. Feeling anxious about Arnie, I deliver the message to its intended ears. Then I try to piece together clues because we've been away for the weekend; I'm concerned that perhaps Louise should have taken Arnie to the emergency room rather than dither around leaving messages for a doctor who was not on call.

———

We're drinking coffee and reading the newspaper in bed on a Saturday morning when the phone rings. I listen to one side of a conversation, but it's enough:

"Hello." . . . "It's no trouble. What's happening?"

"How long have you had the cough?"

"Shortness of breath?" . . . "Have you used your inhalers?" . . . "Fever?"

"Well, it's hard to say without examining you. You know best how you feel, so you can either go to the emergency room now or see me in my office Monday around noon."

"Okay, I'll plan to see you Monday."

From the compartment in my brain that isn't reading the paper, I ask what's going on and my husband fills in the background story: "This patient nearly died with asthma a while ago because she didn't get help soon enough. There wasn't enough oxygen getting to her brain and she was left with memory problems. She has to write notes to herself or she forgets what she's doing. She's your age, has a husband and some kids."

Then I say, "Oh."

Women and Love

She thought she loved, she thought she was full of love.
This was her idea of herself.
—D. H. Lawrence, *Women in Love*

They used to say I looked like her, and I wanted to think it so. In her wedding portrait that hangs on the wall in my dining room, her eyes seem surprisingly confident for one so young, considering that the photo was taken in 1917 when she was twenty years old. But she had already undertaken journeys that might have seemed more daunting than marriage. And besides, she looks like a woman in love, in love with the handsome man who sits in an ornately carved wood chair while she stands in her gown of satin and lace, resting her right forearm on his shoulder.

My grandparents have been there gazing down at family gatherings for years, but I had not bothered to study their faces, had not much contemplated the events leading up to that moment when the shutter opened, until I began paddling through a murky sea of passions with D. H. Lawrence. Troubled by his version of the feminine, I eventually realized that women like my grandmother, consumed by the outright demands of physical *being*, do not rise from the pages of his 1920 novel *Women in Love*. Instead, Lawrence indulges intellectual abstractions—not the "blood knowledge" that he craved in living and writing a man's life—to speculate about women who share certain characteristics with the present-day me: privileged and contemplative and subject to discontent. Feminine hearts such as those he carved for the Brangwen sisters, Gudrun and Ursula, seem to echo rather than pulse, and I feel cheated yet revealed by their inclinations.

Opening the gates to sensual experience, Lawrence probes the schism between mind and body to create women who are fascinated with the *acts* of living, yet oddly unable to integrate them into a fulfilling life. He begins his story with the sisters' thoughts on marriage:

> "You don't think one needs the *experience* of having been married?" [Gudrun] asked.
>
> "Do you think it needs to *be* an experience?" replied Ursula.
>
> "Bound to be, in some way or other," said Gudrun, coolly. "Possibly undesirable, but bound to be an experience of some sort."
>
> "Not really," said Ursula. "More likely to be the end of experience."

Experience? Coolly? What happened to the love Lawrence promised in the title? I wager that my grandmother would have found the sisters' conversation simply silly, as I sometimes do if I'm thinking with my body rather than my mind. Yet that seldom happens these days; I am usually lost in ideas—reading, writing, and imagining how things could be and should be. I suspect that my grandmother would find many aspects of my own pensive, compartmentalized life as baffling as any fictional lives I might share with her.

So I have taken the picture down and placed it on a bench next to the kitchen table, where most important meetings occur in this house, because I want to ask my grandmother about how to live. But looking at the portrait closely, I'm unsettled by the sensual urgency that stirs through the grays and blacks and whites of the captured image. She and my grandfather look so eager and confident, yet on that day neither of them knows that there is a son followed by a daughter in their shared future. Neither of them knows that a doctor will tell them they must leave their friends and relatives in Cleveland and go to the country for fresh air if my grandmother is to recover from an unnamed lung disease. Neither of them knows how back-breakingly hard it will be to support their family by milking cows and raising chickens on a rocky patch of land on the outskirts of a small town in upstate New York. Nor do they know that they will lose every hard-earned possession when their farmhouse burns to the ground. They do not appear the least bit troubled by worry over that which might or might not happen; on that day, they appear ready to leap into their present.

———

Gudrun Brangwen tends to avoid the straightforward approach; she likes to observe her surroundings and then maneuver the possibilities to her best advantage. After studying art in London, she chooses to return to her childhood home in a poor mining town, even though "she loathed it," because she anticipates using familiar ground to launch herself into another phase of life. But in the meantime, she craves sensation, wants to "test the full effect of this shapeless, barren ugliness upon herself." Walking through town to watch a wedding procession, she passes amidst the poor in "a dark, uncreated, hostile world," yet she, like visiting royalty, is drenched in vernal beauty with "her grass-green stockings, her large grass-green velour hat, her full soft coat, of a strong blue colour." The common people in their gritty underworld stare at her and she finds the briefest glimpse of them, "'all soiled, everything sordid,'" horrible and wonderful at once. She remarks on witnessing such lives: "'It's like being mad. . . .'"

As wedding guests stream into the church, Gudrun sees "each one as a complete figure, like a character in a book, or a subject in a picture, or a marionette in a theatre, a finished creation," and she regards them as "sealed and stamped and finished with, for her." And then the bride's "gleaming" brother, Gerald Crich, appears, and his "maleness, like a young, good-humoured, smiling wolf," thrills Gudrun: "He was erect and complete," and she fixates on wanting to see him again. But more urgently, she wants to savor her own erotic response: "She wanted to be alone, to know this strange, sharp inoculation that had changed the whole temper of her blood." With revelation of Gudrun's aggressive appetites and lack of sentimentality, the stage awaits the inevitable encounter and struggle between femme fatale and wolf.

Perhaps the self-absorbed dramas consuming the Brangwen sisters grate at me because I recognize some of my own tendencies to examine *the idea* of desire and *the idea* of love among the living, as if writing my own novel. I only half-jokingly suggest to adventurous young women that their escapades with mildly dangerous men will provide them with something to think about when they are fifty and peeling potatoes at the sink. But the joke stopped being funny when a single friend in her early twenties confided to me that her menstrual period was late, actual flesh had superseded *the idea* of experience, and soon many things seemed dangerously too late. Now, after measuring the past and present across miles of peelings, I seem no closer to knowing how to live a complete life. Can an overly examined life result in a mirror of lonely narcissism? Doesn't one who collects experiences simply have a ragged sack full of stories at the end? Is that what Lawrence inadvertently shows us while immersed in pushing the bounds of love relationships?

I want to believe that my romantic reading of my grandparents' portrait is true, that love undeniably emanates from beneath its crackled surface. But there is another undeniable truth: My grandmother really had no good choice but to find a husband. Anastasia Gajewski spent her early girlhood years near Krakow, where she lived with her parents and several siblings, how many I do not know. The inescapable sorrow of her early life was that her father went to America with the promise of earning money and sending for his family, but the summons never came. So when she was thirteen years old, my grandmother, on her own, boarded a ship bound for New York where she would search for her father. Miraculously, she located him living and working on a Long Island duck farm, but he did not particularly want to be found.

Where did she get the money for the trip? Did she really travel alone? She must have been with someone, wasn't she? How did she know how to get to the duck farm? Did someone help her? Someone must have helped her. I ask my mother these questions, ashamed and sorry that I never asked them of the woman who lived those trials before she died when I was fifteen. My eighty-seven-year-old mother can only reply that my grandmother never wanted to talk about any of it; she does not know why. The family story has always been that she emigrated alone, and that's the way it will remain.

If the girl Anastasia had given over to thinking about her life, she might have been paralyzed with fear, but it seems that she would not be defeated. Leaving her father, she traveled to Cleveland to live with cousins. How did she get there? It must have been by train. Was she still alone? Did she have money? What blood relation connected her to those cousins? Was there an aunt? An uncle? What did she do after she got there? Even though I do so too late, I worry as if I am mother to the girl she was. I press my own mother to remember anything from distant stories, but she has forgotten or perhaps never knew. She offers that my grandmother worked in a restaurant at some point because she sometimes talked about making coffee at her job. Her special recipe was to add broken egg shells to the ground coffee before brewing. So I plump the edges of my family history with this detail from long ago.

Considering the disappointments and difficulties in Anastasia's life, Frank Sleve must have looked like blue-eyed salvation when she met him. Together they might forge a partnership in which two poor immigrants could survive and create a family. No wonder her expression in the portrait is resolute and pleased to display two gold bands encircling the ring finger of her white-gloved right hand. Although I recall her wearing only one gold band during her years as my grandmother, the particular that puzzles me as I look at her image is how those rings could possibly have fit her naked finger if they fit over her gloved one. Then my eyes drift to the ringed finger of her new husband's smooth right hand as it cups his crossed knee. That pose puts his high black shoe into the foreground of the composition, its soft leather pulled into shallow folds by the snug laces at his ankle. Strange to study that foot so finely shod when in life I remember him trudging wearily from the cow barn in dirt-and-manure-encrusted boots, then climbing the wobbly porch stairs that led to the kitchen where she waited with the food she had prepared for him.

No, intellectual speculation about marriage did not concern my grandmother. She was busy working in and on and for a life that was made possible because of her marriage. Moving in silent recollection through the long ago rooms of my grandparents' house, I can sometimes find them sitting in dark upholstered chairs, wearing eyeglasses and reading a newspaper, but I do not see a single book. I remember the excitement when they got a television and we watched the *Ed Sullivan Show* in their living room, beneath the stag's head that peered down from the wall. But mostly I imagine them sitting side by side in the old wooden rocking chairs on the front porch—weary after a long day of milking, feeding, watering, gathering, chopping, shoveling, cooking, cleaning, washing—surrounded by their family and their land.

———

The more I think about my grandmother and love, the more certain I am that Lawrence cared little about a real woman's life. As Gudrun uses the poor villagers for the pleasures of voyeurism, Lawrence uses women in his contemplation of masculine suffering and ecstasy on

earth. Wanting to defy moral codes and plumb the depths of experience, he sends in pasteboard women with sex appeal who manipulate
and demand in order to seize whatever power is within their grasps.
Meanwhile, Lawrence's men find pleasure and pain with these women,
but they desire others as well. Relationship charts for his characters
sound like newspaper personal ads in which man seeks woman, man
seeks man, man seeks self, woman seeks man, and woman seeks self.

Lawrence uses fiction to "test the full effect" of possibilities that
interest him. With musky scents rising from the pages, Gerald Crich
and Rupert Birkin engage in nude jiu-jitsu behind locked doors, wres-
tling "swiftly, rapturously, intent and mindless at last" in a pantomime
of their true desires. The partners attain satisfying "exhaustion" and
the encounter holds "some deep meaning to them"; yet, Gerald shows
he can also "reap the women like a harvest" at a party in Paris where
"'every woman in the room was ready to surrender to him.'" Gudrun
describes her response to Gerald's sexual persona as causing her to
feel like "'a whole roomful of women at once,'" as if she'd "'caught a
Sultan.'" With erotic tension rising, she appears "strange, exotic, sa-
tiric," and dresses for dinner in a "daring gown of vivid green silk and
tissue of gold" that captivates her own crowd of admirers. Meanwhile,
Ursula knows the pleasure of Birkin's "suave perfect loins and thighs
of darkness" amidst the bracken during a night in the woods, and as
their relationship progresses, she decides that there should be no limits on their sexual acts: "Why not be bestial, and go the whole round
of experience? She exulted in it. . . . There would be no shameful thing
she had not experienced."

However, the Brangwen sisters never discuss the "experience" of
pregnancy. Unwanted pregnancies and the burden of societal judgment
the morning after are for flesh and blood women, not the Brangwen
sisters. Consumed with a man's drive to live fully, Lawrence does not
recognize the incarnadine flood of realities in the *lived* lives of ordinary women. Instead, he gratuitously consigns an out-of-wedlock
pregnancy to a beautiful, promiscuous, oyster-eating artist's model

called Pussum who "accepts her position as a social inferior" and intends to trap her man into marriage: "She wanted him completely in her power. Then she would marry him." *What does this tableau mean in real time?*

———

When poor women get bestial, it's with blood, sweat, and consequences. Take my parents' cousins. One of them apparently couldn't say no to herself—nor to her husband's boss, the heating oil delivery man, her daughter's boyfriend, the boyfriend's uncle, and a long line of manly bar patrons, wedding revelers, and funeral mourners. Her children bear little resemblance to each other, and she botched a coat-hanger-abortion one spring day (according to my weeping grandmother who spilled the story to me when I was ten and we were walking home from an evening Lenten service). Another cousin, who favored jet black hair dye and thick layers of cheap make-up, repeatedly said yes to men in uniform, particularly state troopers. Elevating her sex life into the realm of charity work, she proclaimed, "I serve the needy not the greedy." And yet another cousin described the embarrassment of owning up to a willing older sister referred to as the "Town Pump," who surprisingly gave birth to only two illegitimate children (one fathered by a married man), surrendering each for adoption.

The first woman, now in her seventies with hands gnarled by arthritis and short gray hair burnt by home permanents, lives alone; but, her name raises old stories about parties at hunting cabins, reckless women, and rough men capable of slipping a Mickey here and there to mix things up. The second (the sexual philanthropist) died with neither chick nor child, as my mother would say. And the third collects giraffe trinkets, wears leopard print pant suits, and carries a cell phone to stay in touch with her aging truck-driver lover whose boxer shorts rest beneath her pillow while he's on the road. A young woman contacted her several years ago saying that she wanted to meet her birth mother, but was soon told that the desire for a mother/daughter relationship was not mutual. Tallying these scorecards, my sister and I once debated which woman was the family's most experienced whore.

Although my life has been far more sheltered and restrained—in countless ways—than those lived by the cousins, my grandmother could not have imagined my experiences since her death. I left that impoverished town of her adulthood and my childhood to study at a large university. Terrified, confused, and surrounded by throngs of students far more worldly than I, I looked and felt as if I had just fallen from a hay wagon. She who had sewn dresses for herself out of printed muslin chicken-feed bags might have nodded proudly at the dress of sturdy brown cotton dotted with sprays of lavender flowers that I had sewn for college. She would have seen evidence of my mother's good sense in the grocery carton packed with bread, peanut butter, and home canned peaches floating in sealed Mason jars, one grooved peach pit at the bottom of each. But then she would have wondered over the gradual disappearance of things and ways that I had brought with me from home, and been shocked at the tiny ribbed sweaters, tight jeans, and miniskirts that took over my closet. Most of all, the men that I dated, some of whom I thought I loved, would have caused her disappointment and concern.

———

Lawrence imagines Ursula nearest to happiness when she believes that she has lassoed her man Birkin in a relationship based on consuming, mutual desire, but her ideals crumple with the discovery that she's not enough: For completeness, Birkin wants "'eternal union with a man too: another kind of love.'" Meanwhile, Gudrun embodies female decadence and discontent as she barters herself through a progression of perceived gains. She and Gerald engage in "this eternal see-saw, one destroyed that the other might exist, one ratified because the other was nulled." He feels tortured in their relationship, but sees that she is unfeeling and "sufficient unto herself, closed round and completed, like a thing in a case."

So Gudrun contemplates possibilities for new sensations as she finds herself attracted to Loerke, a sculptor from Dresden who has known poverty, a "mud-child" who "seemed to be the very stuff of the underworld of life." She begins to negotiate the gauntlet separating them, yet, at twenty-six, her challenge seems insurmountable since Loerke's proclaimed ideal of feminine beauty fixates on women younger than twenty who are "'small and fresh and tender and slight.'" But after he explains that love is detestable, and that he seeks a higher relationship in which "'it is the *me* that is looking for a mistress, and my *me* is waiting for the thee of the mistress, for the match to my particular intelligence,'" Gudrun anticipates that she might fit nicely into that abstract, feminine role. Loerke's admission of physically abusing a seventeen-year-old girl who modeled for him and his current relationship with a young, male "love-companion" only add to his intrigue in Gudrun's eyes. Without the traditional tethers of love, she imagines a relationship with the artist as "a fine game" that would not impinge on her freedom: "One will escape from so much, that is the chief thing, escape so much hideous boring repetition of vulgar actions, vulgar phrases, vulgar postures." Gudrun sees any man who interests her as but one possible option for her next move.

———

Lawrence seems to anticipate a feminine discontent that I had imagined flaming into existence during the women's rights movement of the 1960s and 70s, the years when birth control pills finally became available to married *and* unmarried women, the era during which I was a college student. On a summer evening when I was twenty years old and halfway to becoming a nurse, I ended a two-year relationship with my high school French teacher by returning his engagement ring with empty apologies. No longer shocking, no longer secret, the fact that we were a couple had grown boring; my *me* wanted entanglements with men who were neither like him nor like the small-town boys I'd known.

When I returned to campus the next fall, my dating game got off to a rocky start with Tuna, a party animal who joined his fraternity brothers in getting stoned for a group trip to see *Fantasia*, then afterwards took me directly back to my dorm because I so clearly wasn't any fun. A few months later, I agreed to attend a basketball game with another fraternity boy who served as the university mascot, but I hadn't expected him to appear at my dorm in full costume. I silently accepted that I was stuck with the Saltine Warrior for the evening, and rode off to the field house where I watched him rally the fans with war dances and tomahawk antics. These were not the experiences I craved.

Then there was Bob who didn't mind cheating on his girlfriend from home as he satisfied his own cravings for experience. But I was sure that I loved him; I waited for calls that didn't come, and I was way too grateful when he drove back to campus from his cottage in Canada to surprise me at my summer sublet. And he did; I had all but given up on him. There had been a lonely stretch and I sometimes ate dinner with his friend Steve, even though he had a girlfriend Nadine in another city. During those evenings, Steve mostly reviewed why he and I should not become romantically entangled when we nearly did, and tried to convince me that his roommate Mike was really the nice guy for me. But with Bob's unexpected return, my life was his: I cooked our meals, washed his clothes, melted into his eyes, and hid in the closet with him, giggling, while a grad student who thought he loved me pounded on the apartment door, shouting that I should let him in so we could talk. None of those experiences worked out.

I wondered if I might make something of handsome Joe whose dark moods marked him as lost and in need of saving—that is, until he drifted away. Harry from Long Island was a medical student who wore a long camel-hair overcoat whenever weather permitted (and sometimes when it didn't), and we went to the Grand Prix at Watkins

Glen together. For a few slow weeks, we went out for drinks and played foosball only to find that the thrill was gone. I hit an all-time low when I dated a red Corvette convertible and pretended to like eating raw clams with its cruel man until I became too frightened of him to continue. But a different Mike, who also knew Bob, presented interesting possibilities and I had begun to hope that he would ask me out. And he might have if I hadn't quite suddenly married.

I had fallen in love. Following a first date during September of my senior year, life took shape according to the progression of the affair: We disentangled ourselves from other relationships, lived together for three months, found a church, ordered a cake, invited our families to our wedding, said our "I do's," flew away on a honeymoon, and, six months later, went to my college graduation. There is undeniable truth in this romantic rendition of love and marriage, but there is another undeniable truth: I was afraid of the woman I might become without a husband. I did not know how to calibrate the freedoms of mind and body in such a way that the single *me* was not perpetually at risk.

An educated version of my mother's cousins? Unwanted pregnancies, adoption farewells, abortions? A collection of experiences? Instead I chose a life not unlike my grandmother's in that I worked in and on and for my marriage and family. Yet, the insistent demands of that contained world diminished an inner spirit that dared not demand attention. I did not know how to balance the pieces, and it could be argued that while Lawrence's Brangwen sisters err towards the conceptual (as "characters" can), I steered toward reality until my children were grown. Then I once again became fascinated by intellectual abstraction and possibilities.

So, "like a thing in a case," I have constructed compartments in which the wife me, mother me, daughter me, and writer me attempt to function in relative isolation from each other much of the time. Thinking, reading, writing, and manipulating versions of reality: My grandmother probably would not understand my system—any more than she would understand D. H. Lawrence. But, as I find myself far from my beginnings, Ursula and Gudrun nudge each of those women that I am to question the choices made during the progression of a female life. I imagine my grandmother wondering why I care about those fictional characters who crave sensation and experience. She would prefer glimpses of that girl, the unknowing and vulnerable soft thing, who looks to her grandmother for answers about how to live. She might suspect that, like her, the girl was saved by love.

———

When I return the portrait to its hook, I study my grandmother's bouquet of open-petaled roses—those of a sort that can insist their loveliness from a wild tangle of thorns draped across a stone wall. Frilly ferns and long, pale ribbons mingle with the flowers and drip nearly to the toe of my grandfather's high black shoe. Her hair parts on the right, like mine, and she has fastened it up under loose ruffles of veil that cascade from beneath a wreath of more blowsy flowers and tiny-leafed vines. And still more blossoms cluster in a corsage pinned over her heart. I wonder if he placed it there, against her breast, and fiddled clumsily with a pin while glancing into her eyes. He must have, because they are beautiful, these two, with their ready flesh barely disguised by their wedding clothes. Yes, my grandmother looks like a woman in love.

Hot Stuff

> [Q]uite possibly, behind the awful juvenile clichés, there was in her
> a garden and a twilight, and a palace gate. . . .
> —Vladimir Nabokov, *Lolita*

I recently finished re-reading *Lolita* and started thinking again about how we moderns of the Western world nuzzle our fantasy-filled desires. Nabokov knew that most of us are fascinated by the forbidden possibilities in our erotic thoughts, even though responsible, raised-on-guilt citizens recognize the little voice that recommends a cold shower—for the good of the soul, for the good of society. In choosing the big pedophilia taboo and the hints of incest that course through *Lolita*, he meant to shock us into thinking about the daily, nightly, non-stop collisions of fantasy and reality. What about indulgence of those desires that ask to be hidden in shadows? What happens when emotional truth demands a reckoning? Not to suggest censoring the imagination, after all, a costumed cast of characters dancing through conjured lives can be life-sustaining. Still, I wonder about our desires, and the deceits they generate when we impose them on others.

I tried framing a simple entry to critical analysis of Nabokov's text with a question: Who's the pervert? I suppose I was trying to be glib with that maneuver, but I found that the answer isn't so simple. Consider the obvious: Humbert Humbert, the novel's middle-aged protagonist/memoirist who was born in Paris and raised on the Riviera, is a self-proclaimed madman with a passion for young girls of a very particular type, and about whom he considers himself an expert. Consider Humbert's idea of female perfection: "Between the age limits of nine and fourteen there occur maidens who, to certain bewitched travelers, twice or many times older than they, reveal their true nature which is not human, but nymphic (that is, demoniac); and these chosen creatures I propose to designate as 'nymphets.'" This leads to twelve-year-old Dolores Haze who flirts shamelessly with Humbert, identifies herself as "'a friend to male animals,'" and admits to being "'absolutely filthy in thought, word and deed.'" Of course there's also Nabokov, a fifty-six-year-old-man in 1955 when his infamous tale of obsession was published amidst debate over whether art or smut had been served. And last but not least, there's me, a hopelessly devoted *Lolita* reader, five years old when the book first appeared in print, and now a very particular woman who's been bewitched by Humbert during four (perhaps five, maybe six) separate engagements over the past nine years. *I touch my eyes and my lips to the opening lines—* "Lolita, light of my life, fire of my loins. My sin, my soul."—*and I can no more resist their invitation than the nympholept can turn from* "the slightly feline outline of a cheekbone, the slenderness of a downy limb."

I like to claim that a passion for language explains my obsession with *Lolita*; Nabokov's word liquor seduces me to a realm of pleasure and pain where taboos are for other people. I flutter from one phrase to another, sipping perfect lyricism and nibbling on raw lust, wanting to be surprised by verbal beauty that is itself eroticized by elements of surprise. A trip to the park with Humbert, where he sits on a "rack of joy" to feast on little girl visions, should disgust me, but turns delicious instead. I, a she-bear of a mother in reality, never consider calling the police as Humbert describes his secret raptures:

> How marvelous were my fancied adventures as I sat on a hard park bench pretending to be immersed in a trembling book. Around the quiet scholar, nymphets played freely, as if he were a familiar statue or part of an

old tree's shadow and sheen. Once a perfect little beauty in a tartan frock, with a clatter put her heavily armed
foot near me upon the bench to dip her slim bare arms
into me and tighten the strap of her roller skate, and I
dissolved in the sun, with my book for fig leaf. . . .

Humbert makes a wish upon his petite morsels—"Let them play around me forever. Never grow up."—but later wonders: "In this wrought-iron world of criss-cross cause and effect, could it be that the hidden throb I stole from them did not affect *their* future?" A test of personal power rather than a pang of conscience would seem to be the likely impetus behind this "great and terrible" line of questioning, yet, Humbert's pause over the raveling of fate triggers my own confronta-tion with the weave of fantasy and reality. *Do we choose our fantasies, or do they choose us? Does the sheer energy of a gaze, desiring or merely fascinated, change the unaware subject? Or do I mean object?*

During the long ago summer of 1923, Humbert shared mutu-al passion with Annabel, his first love who was only a few months younger than his own thirteen years. She died of typhus four months later, but the female fantasy image that Humbert carries into adult-hood remains fixed on her physical body—as it was before she became his "dead bride." When he recalls his actual, brief marriage during young adulthood to Valeria, a woman "at least in her late twenties" who "pouted, and dimpled, and romped," he explains it as an attempt to put "a soothing presence" in his life. With his live bride wearing a child's nightshirt that he had stolen from an orphanage, Humbert admits that he had "some fun from that nuptial night and had the idiot in hysterics by sunrise," but he soon realized that he "had on his hands a large, puffy, short-legged, big-breasted and practically brain-less *baba*." No, Humbert wants "*fruit vert*," the underage female whom our society deems sexually off limits, and with whom his relations will always be experientially asymmetric. The adult man craves the impos-sible: A frozen-in-time-girl-child who is a coequal lover.

Sandra Swinburne

The summer of 1947 finds Humbert recently checked out of a psychiatric sanatorium, and traveling to Ramsdale, New Hampshire where he plans to rent a room from a couple with two daughters whom he "would coach in French and fondle in Humbertish." On discovering that the family's house was destroyed by fire, he agrees to consider the home of Charlotte Haze, an attractive woman in her thirties who hopes that he will become the gentleman lodger in her spare room. Humbert accompanies the lady of the house on a domestic tour and spies her daughter Dolores sunbathing in the backyard (which the ever-aspiring Charlotte calls "'the piazza'") with a "polka-dotted black kerchief tied around her chest." Seeing the girl "half-naked, kneeling, turning about on her knees," memory allows Humbert to know Annabel's living body once more:

> And, as if I were the fairy-tale nurse of some little princess (lost, kidnaped, discovered in gypsy rags through which her nakedness smiled at the king and his hounds), I recognized the tiny dark-brown mole on her side. With awe and delight (the king crying for joy, the trumpets blaring, the nurse drunk) I saw again her lovely indrawn abdomen where my south-bound mouth had briefly paused; and those puerile hips on which I had kissed the crenulated imprint left by the band of her shorts—that last mad immortal day behind the "Roches Roses." The twenty-five years I had lived since then, tapered to a palpitating point, and vanished.

Imaginative flight transports Humbert through time and space and nothing matters but the merging of his lost Annabel with this found Lolita. Overwhelmed by beauty and desire and the compulsion to repeat, Humbert enters "the breathless garden" on knees that seem "like reflections of knees in rippling water."

The Last Good Obsession

I am an irredeemable watcher and my motives are not necessarily without erotic intent; I like thinking about how each of us inhabits a physical body, how we mingle and respond to each other. I study my prey and then imagine their stories—sometimes take my pleasure from talking and writing about them. That's my explanation for why I went to the George Eastman House Museum to see nearly six hundred publicity photos of performers from Palace Burlesque, an establishment that once stood at 327 Main Street in Buffalo, New York. An exhibit called "The Tease: Burlesque Performers from the 1950s & '60s" displayed eight by ten glossies of voluptuous women who were shimmying through real-man fantasies while the fictional Humbert complained to early readers of feeling "strangulated" by taboos, and attempted to reason pedophilia into rightness with the argument that young girls had inspired Dante and Petrarch.

The female body as an object of beauty and desire raises questions about perception and experience of both *beauty* and *desire*. Staring at photos of nearly nude women ornamented with rosebud pasties, sequinned garter belts, fishnet stockings, and deftly placed feathers, I found many of them beautiful, while others seemed pathetic in their apparent eagerness to please. Like Humbert suspended in examination of his own voyeuristic pleasures, I wondered about the dynamic created by watching eyes—beholder and beheld. I studied the considerable weight of Virginia Ding Dong Bell's melon-sized breasts, studied the way they once strained the seams of a scanty black corset, and I watched men, who were clearly there to see art, pay homage to their twin magnificence. Was their fascination doing harm? Was mine? Does ogling the photograph of the au natural woman who sits inside a jumbo cocktail glass, like a cherry or an olive waiting to be consumed, certify the female body as a commodity?

What did Zsa-Zsa Cortez, Ineda Mann, and Sin-Tana—each so foxy on paper—think about while performing live bump and grind for a room full of hungry eyes besides the money they were earning? What imaginative fuel sent a woman called Tinker Bell to the stage wearing a barely-there Cleopatra costume, or inspired Sunny Day the Butterfly Goddess to flap the gauzy wings attached to her arms? An audience photograph shows men dressed in suits and neckties sitting at tables with cigarettes and drinks, like a scene from an old movie. Did their spellbound gazes somehow vitalize Wow-Wow as she shook her tassels, or quicken Naughty Valetta's pulse as she swirled her long cape like the evil queen from fairy tales? Were marriages crowded by the fantasies that customers took home? The same photo also records the presence of a few sedately clothed women in the audience. Did they wonder how their own femaleness stacked up against the hyper-sexualized strippers? Perhaps there was something for everyone in that room: In *On Beauty and Being Just*, Elaine Scarry proposes that during visual experience of beauty, a "key source of continuity between beholder and beheld" rests in "the way each affirms the aliveness of the other."

The *Buffalo News* posted an online article by Colin Dabkowski about the stripper exhibit at the Eastman House in which he refers to the once thriving Palace Burlesque enterprise as an example of live gender theater that could not survive the increased availability of pornography. Robert and Nina Freudenheim purchased the collection of performer photographs (of the sort that were "kept secretly by millions of American men") after the final show at the Palace in 1977. Stating in an interview with Dabkowski that the photos "'really tell a story about a lot of things,'" Ms. Freudenheim recalls having worked at an advertising agency in Buffalo during the 1950s for a boss who disappeared each Friday afternoon with the excuse that he was having late lunch. "'He came back in such a good mood,'" that everyone in the office knew he was lying; instead, he had been at the Palace for the two o'clock strip show. Although the lunch ruse seems silly in Freudenheim's retelling, there's also a macho glow about the boss' indulgence in erotic pay-for-view. Perhaps a broad awareness that desire makes fools of us all protects him from seeming more exploitative, or more pitiful.

The experience of beauty during Palace performances was sanctioned by a sort of unwritten contract. Advertisements from the era claimed that the shows went beyond the imagination, the strippers accepted money for visual access to their bodies, and audience members bought looking rights that would likely result in imagined sexual acts. Participants in that fantasia might serve as living proof of Elaine Scarry's assertion: "[W]hen the eye sees someone beautiful, the whole body wants to reproduce the person." She explains that perceived beauty indeed "prompts the begetting of children," but a scaled back expression of the replication urge is "the everyday fact of staring" in an attempt to sustain the pleasurable image. Yet, there's something sleazy about those take-it-off events at the Palace, even under the presumption that all parties were consenting adults. *And are the strippers teaching me anything about Humbert's particularly sticky situation involving nymphets, when, even though he does not touch, he looks and lusts without permission?*

Scarry acknowledges two political postures critical of attention to beauty, one based on arguments that it diverts concern from "wrong social arrangements" (concern that could perhaps transform those constructs), and the other built on claims that the act of staring to prolong beauty's spell is in fact a selfish behavior that harms the recipient of the attention. But she finds the logic of those beliefs flawed, and responds by asking whether attention to deserving things that are not beautiful would in turn harm them. For me, the important insight into the morality of looking at nymphets and strippers comes from Scarry's consideration of the dynamic between beauty and being fair in which she quotes John Rawl's interpretation of fairness as "'symmetry of everyone's relations to each other.'" When the power relation between human beholder and human beheld is markedly unequal—paying customer and scantily clad working woman (who must provide a desired level of sexual titillation in order to remain employed), or lusting adult male and female child—does visual purchase of beauty slip into perversity? Does absence of relationship symmetry result in victimization? What about the strippers' photographs, symmetry of relations, and privileged me? *I'm really just looking at cultural history, no harm done. Really.*

———

Once installed in the Haze household, Humbert immerses himself in the study of Lolita and confesses to his diary that "the thousand eyes wide open in my eyed blood" all focus on her: Skin ("oh, marvelous: tender and tanned"), scent ("I do love that intoxicating brown fragrance of hers"), and movements ("wiggly looseness below the knee"). When his Lolita is troubled by "a speck of something" in her eye, he presses his tongue to its watery surface to lick it clean. Leaving his bedroom door open as an invitation, she rewards his steady attentions with a visit, sits on his knee, and waits for something to happen "with curiosity and composure." Humbert compares himself to a spider, weaving a web through the Haze household, waiting for the moment when he would catch his "beautiful warm-colored prey." But his little beauty weaves her own web as she tests the powers of her body to flummox the man her mother so clearly wants.

Lolita's forwardness in the course of daily life allows Humbert to reap lascivious benefits while each of them feigns innocence: She sprawls on the sofa with her legs across his lap, and he steals "the honey of a spasm without impairing the morals of a minor. Absolutely no harm done." But Humbert is aware of his reliance on fantasy projection, and admits to using objectification to get what he wants: "What I had madly possessed was not she, but my own creation, another, fanciful Lolita—perhaps more real than Lolita; overlapping, encasing her; floating between me and her, and having no will, no consciousness—indeed, no life of her own." Humbert knows that his dreamgirl-lover cannot exist in reality; although he had "fallen in love with Lolita forever," time would take her from him, "she would not be forever Lolita." Just the same, he wants what he wants—but what Lolita wants is less clear.

Humbert crafts desperate plots in his desire to make forbidden fantasy become touchable, feastable flesh, and his creator/accomplice arranges for details to fall in place. Charlotte writes a love letter to the gentleman she imagines Humbert to be and risks offending his "old-world reticence" and "sense of decorum" with a proposal of marriage. Seeing her as a means of securing access to his heart's genuine delight (who is away at summer camp), he accepts the proposal. Humbert tries to cast Charlotte as "my Lolita's big sister" in preparation for his sexual duties, but the adult woman's "heavy hips, round knees, ripe bust, the coarse pink skin of her neck" present distasteful challenges. He reports an attempt to focus on the biologic link between mother and daughter as he "wielded" his "brand-new large-as-life wife." Then he turns to Charlotte's girlhood photo album, hopes to imagine her as she once was, and admits that "it was still a nymphet's scent that in despair I tried to pick up, as I bayed through the undergrowth of dark decaying forest." Fantasies fail to transform Humbert's miserable reality and, not a moment too soon, Charlotte dies when hit by a car in front of her house—just after discovering her new groom's X-rated diary.

Humbert retrieves Lolita from camp with the story that her mother is seriously ill, but instead of going home, he drives toward a hotel where they'll spend their first private night together. He knows of his purported resemblance to "some crooner or actor chap on whom Lo has a crush," and he sometimes reminds himself of her status as "a twelve-year-old child." Yet when she tests her provocative powers, as the gathering currents in her body demand—"'Fact I've been revolt-ingly unfaithful to you, but it does not matter one bit, because you've stopped caring for me anyway'"—he delivers the kiss she requests, taking "tiny sips" from "her hot, opening lips." Humbert then reflects on the shaky state of desire between unequal players:

I knew, of course, it was but an innocent game on her part, a bit of back-fisch foolery in imitation of some simulacrum of fake romance, and since (as the psychotherapist, as well as the rapist, will tell you) the limits and rules of such girlish games are fluid, or at least too childishly subtle for the senior partner to grasp—I was dreadfully afraid I might go too far and cause her to start back in revulsion and terror.

The stage is set for the reader to be appalled by explicit acts of pedophilia, but Nabokov undermines that one-dimensional response. Humbert begs the reader to stay: "Imagine me; I shall not exist if you do not imagine me; try to discern the doe in me, trembling in the forest of my own iniquity; let's even smile a little." Lolita's seductive behavior—childish curiosity or womanish desire—becomes his justification for turning forbidden fantasy into reality, beginning with the morning after their first night in the same bed: "Frigid gentlewomen of the jury! I had thought that months, perhaps years, would elapse before I dared to reveal myself to Dolores Haze; but by six she was wide awake, and by six fifteen we were technically lovers. I am going to tell you something very strange: it was she who seduced me." He later adds, ". . . I was not even her first lover."

———

During my most recent encounter with Humbert, I couldn't help but notice a report on the front page of the *Rochester Democrat and Chronicle*. The headline announces that a "predator" was sentenced to sixteen years in prison, and beneath it, the empty eyes of a handsome, dark-haired man stare from a small photograph.

Marian and his wife owned a gymnastics training center where aspiring child-athletes prepared for competitions—until he was accused of using the internet to seduce a thirteen-year-old female student and then engaging in sexual acts with her at the gym. Now forty-one, Marian is quoted in the newspaper as having told the girl: "'I want to make one thing clear: Never did I have the thoughts to hurt you or your family.'" His reported claim is that their relations "had been blown out of proportion." Having initially accepted a bargain for ten years in jail, Marian was sent back to court after the judge responded to a plea from the girl's parents for more severe punishment. I clipped the article because this man coached my friend's now adult daughter who spent a portion of her childhood at my house, playing hide-and-go-seek on summer evenings and giggling through sleepovers with my own children.

I used to joke with my friend about the gym culture that seemed strange to both of us. The most disciplined of the wiry girl tumblers (some of them with Olympic circles dancing in their eyes) looked so unreal with their hair pulled and fastened tightly away from their faces—all skin, bone, and muscle—that I called them the "Little Aliens." Lightness plus strength makes a winning combination in that sport, so physical growth looms as a sort of enemy to be controlled; flipping around in mid-air and landing upright isn't for large-breasted, broad-hipped girls. Remembering the lean bodies of those gymnasts, my mind wanders to Humbert's erotic taste: "'You should try to be a little nicer to me, Lolita. You should also watch your diet. The tour of your thigh, you know, should not exceed seventeen and a half inches. More might be fatal (I was kidding, of course).'"

My friend's daughter was serious but not crazed over gymnastics, which meant that she trained hard while maintaining other interests. When she competed on the high school team, I went to a couple meets; I closed my eyes during some of the flying vaults, then told my friend that she was a bad mother for allowing her child to participate in something so dangerous. That could be said and we could both laugh because each of us knows that she is a fanatically protective parent who was always in the stands for her children's activities. The news about Marian stunned both mother and daughter into silence;

they trusted him, they liked him and his family, and they only knew his behavior to be professional and supportive.

The "predator" was an accomplished Bulgarian gymnast, and I found his name on a few internet sites for men's world rankings in artistic gymnastics. He and his slender wife, also a former competitive gymnast, had come to America and worked their way up through coaching positions. Then, as sometimes happens, something *did* happen in that shadow world of desire. That something resulted in Marian being accused, found guilty, and locked away.

———

When I was thirteen, my father decided to have an in-ground swimming pool installed, and I was quietly but blissfully aware of having the only one for miles around. Never mind that the low-slung storage shed full of equipment for my father's roofing and siding business served as the poolside cabana. Slathered in baby oil, I lounged beside the water reading *Teen* magazine and dreaming myself Hollywood tan, save the wide stripe concealed by my swimsuit. That happened a long time ago, in a one-beer-joint town surrounded by luckless farms, behind my family's small house next to the parking lot of the local kindergarten through twelfth-grade school.

The third floor windows of the principal's office overlooked my backyard resort, as did the windows of two boys' bathrooms. Aging janitors lumbered in and out of the building; middle-aged mechanics greased and oiled the fleet of yellow buses in the garage at the end of the lot; book-toting teachers came and went. Only once do I remember a boy hooting from a window at my cousin and me as we lounged in our swimsuits, and we simply laughed. For a few years, I gave little thought to the possibilities and implications of being looked at as a sexual object. Not until I was a seventeen-year-old senior in high school, and totally bored by the local boys I knew, did I have burning reason to consciously pose next to my pool and in plenty of other places as well.

During my teenaged years, I imagined escape from that town with a mix of eagerness and outright fear. My parents believed that girls should have educations that would result in jobs, should they ever need to work, in case marriages went wrong, so I had begun making plans for college during my junior year in high school with the insulated assumption that my choice was between nursing and teaching. After deciding on a Bachelor of Science degree in nursing, I looked at state schools where tuition costs were reasonable. But September of my senior year introduced an unexpected influence: The new French teacher was male, tall, not unattractive, and a fresh graduate of Syracuse University. Furthermore, he'd studied at the Sorbonne during a semester in Paris, and he brought French rock and roll records to class. I remember borrowing a Sylvie Vartan album from him. *Why do I remember that detail when so many others have simply vanished?*

I began dressing to appear older and studied like mad trying to insure that I would do well in French. Sitting near the back of the basement room where class met, I seldom made eye contact with the object of my fantasies, just the occasional coy glance and smile unless I was called upon. Early in the semester, my French teacher saw that I was a good student and encouraged me to apply to the nursing program at Syracuse, tempting me with notions that I'd be "only a step below the Ivy League." By winter, I was going to high school basketball games, walking in late so as not to seem adolescently eager, but also because he coached the junior varsity team and I wanted him to notice me. Without doing anything overt that could be pinned on me (*But the eyes tell all, don't you think?*), I silently stalked the new teacher whom I imagined as a sophisticated man of the world; after all, he'd studied at the Sorbonne.

In March, he phoned me at home, just to talk, and a few days later, phoned again. By April, he was driving from the nearby town where he lived, just to stop in, on Saturday, after dark, with all the window shades drawn in my living room. My parents didn't see anything wrong with our romance, reasoning that I was *nearly* eighteen and he was only five years older. They somehow thought that his visits were nobody else's business; for all anyone knew, he might be calling on them, not me. But they weren't kissing him at the door when he left the house, then sitting in his class each school day with a secret tucked away, hoping that nobody—the principal or another teacher or another student or a cook or a janitor—would mention anything about inappropriate relationships.

After the June graduation ceremony, my parents invited a few people over for dinner. I had scored a perfect one hundred on the statewide French exam, and I remember hearing my teacher proudly report that fact to someone standing on the back porch of my house that night. I silently wondered if any errors had been overlooked when he graded the test. Former student and teacher smiled at each other, but carefully avoided physical contact. The following day, the shades were raised on our dating, and he appeared at my house several times each week to go for a swim or to the movies or for a drive. Our romance had survived and we had somehow escaped public censoring by school and town. Looking back, I suspect that my father's blustering personality and relative financial success intimidated those who might have suspected what was going on, thereby saving me from disgrace.

I left home that fall to attend Syracuse University where I struggled to belong while feeling like a hick and a misfit. None of the fraternities asked me to be a little sister and I pretended not to care; that nonsense was for the rich, really pretty girls. I stayed in the dorm most evenings with the other girls who either had boyfriends back home or never had dates. I was intimidated by the students who seemed so worldly and smart and no doubt gave them reason to laugh at how gullible I could be. Why do I remember Susan from Albany asking me to pronounce *s-u-a-v-e* and then laughing after I did so, correcting me to emphasize a long vowel *a* rather than the short vowel sound I had used? Her joke was to convince me that a mispronunciation was correct, and I dropped into the trap, dead weight. I assumed she was right and I was wrong, assumed I'd heretofore made a blunder each time *suave* had passed my lips. Feeling stupid I took comfort in knowing that at least I had an older guy showing up to see me nearly every weekend. My arrangement was a bit risqué and exciting—made me interesting; no freshman boys for me. By summer I was wearing an engagement ring and my French teacher-boyfriend found a job near Syracuse so we could see each other more often.

But by the end of sophomore year, I was sick of studying and sulking in my room while others dated and partied. I didn't want to waste another year of college cooking dinner for a fiancé who no longer talked about the Sorbonne; I didn't want to chaperone another minute of another high school dance in the small town down Route 31 where he had taken a job to be near me. I wanted to have fun. Dormitory life had taught me something about more stylish clothes and make-up, and I longed to test my skill in the marketplace. Feeling like I'd deceived a nice person whom I liked but didn't love into believing I was a mature someone I wasn't, I finally found the courage to return the diamond ring one summer day before my junior year began. *He's weeping, holding the ring in its box, asking are you sure, are you sure, and I'm saying I'm sure, I'm sure.* Afterwards, I was relieved one moment, but convinced the next that I'd ruined two lives. I felt like a fallen woman when I returned to school, bruised but wanting, so I played the part: I taught myself how to smoke cigarettes in front of a dormitory mirror, prowled the campus bar circuit swilling beer from long-necked bottles, and imagined myself as hot stuff.

⁓

Each time I re-enter the heaven and hell of Humbert's life, he shows me that he's a monster who sustains a one-track drive to recapture long ago ecstasy by imagining reality transformed: ". . . I would take a bed-and-cot or twin-bed cabin, a prison cell of paradise, with yellow window shades pulled down to create a morning illusion of Venice and sunshine when actually it was Pennsylvania and rain." Hop-scotching between cabins, motels, and hotels during a year on the run, he juggles bribery and terror to control a Lolita who relies on sexual reluctance, affectations of ennui, and wisecracks to even the score. When she seems pliant, he rewards her with trinkets and privileges—even piles on the gifts to keep her in tow after he tells her that her mother is actually dead, not sick:

> In the gay town of Lepingville I bought her four books of comics, a box of candy, a box of sanitary pads, two cokes, a manicure set, a travel clock with a luminous dial, a ring with a real topaz, a tennis racket, roller skates with white high shoes, field glasses, a portable radio set, chewing gum, a transparent raincoat, sunglasses, some more garments—swooners, shorts, all kinds of summer frocks.

But when she becomes defiant in her so called "moodiness," he threatens her with possible banishment to an Appalachian farm, or dramatizes the horrors of detention in a reformatory—all of which he recollects "with the deepest moan of shame."

Humbert guards his Lolita, and watches jealously for any sign of infidelity, pouncing on the slightest clue with enraged accusations. Finding her captor cruel but ridiculous, she replies to one such episode with, "'You must be confusing me with some other fast little article,'" which only causes him to wallow in self-pity and think her heartless. He may tell himself that the imagined "Annabel Haze, alias Dolores Lee, alias Loleeta" does not really exist, and that Dolores Haze does not love him—"Never did she vibrate under my touch. . ."—but he finds himself hopelessly addicted, "[for] there is no other bliss on earth comparable to that of fondling a nymphet." On a bed of wildflowers next to a mountain stream, Humbert conjures a visit from Venus as he recalls having sex with his girl-captive—who weeps while he holds her. Not until long after their travels are over, does he admit in his memoir to being the cause of "her sobs in the night—every night, every night— the moment I feigned sleep."

Queasy from the depravity of Humbert's demands, I usually feel excited at reaching the part when Dolores runs away with the visiting author of her school play. I'm not happy about the sordid bargain she makes with another adult male to win some measure of self-deter-mination, but Humbert deserves to suffer. Then after three years of life without her, Humbert receives a "Dear Dad" letter from Dolly Haze Schiller because she's married, pregnant, and poor; she asks for money, adding that she has "gone through much sadness and hard-ship." He finds her living in "a clapboard shack, with two or three similar ones farther away from the road and a waste of withered weeds all around." When he recalls their reunion, he includes "her ruined looks and her adult, rope-veined narrow hands and her goose-flesh white arms, and her shallow ears, and her unkempt armpits, there she was (my Lolita!), hopelessly worn at seventeen. . . ." *And that scene is a reality I feared. I know those forsaken roads that give way to the occasional dirt driveways leading to trailers with built-on-sheds or to rotting frame houses covered with sheets of silver insulation not siding. Rusted pickup trucks, old tires, broken appliances, and broken furniture pile up in the yards where some of my schoolmates have spent their lives with dulled eyes and teeth that come out at night. If I'd failed to take my ticket out of town when I was seventeen, could a life amidst "withered weeds" have been mine?*

In spite of all I know of life and fiction, in spite of having wit-nessed Humbert's self-serving lies, I still take a tumble each time I encounter his insistence that he loves Lolita: "It was love at first sight, at last sight, at ever and ever sight." He claims that he no longer needs his nymphet fantasies: "I insist the world know how much I loved my Lolita, *this* Lolita, pale and polluted, and big with another's child, but still gray-eyed, still sooty-lashed, still auburn and almond, still Carmencita, still mine. . . ." And I want to believe him. But in falling for Humbert's story, I not only want to believe in love, I want to believe in the possibility of redemption. My favorite part of the novel comes when he describes standing on a hillside where "the melody of children at play" rises from a valley below. I love looking across the stream and treetops and rooftops and almost hearing the "almost articulate spurt of laughter, or the crack of a bat, or the clatter of a toy wagon." Humbert writes that "the hopelessly poignant thing was not Lolita's absence from my side, but the absence of her voice from that concord," and I will that recognition of moral truth to be real. Serving time for killing the man he blames for stealing Lolita from him, he admits no remorse for murder, but willingly concedes that he deserves "at least thirty-five years for rape."

———

Of course Nabokov knew he was playing with fire while imagining *Lolita* into being. His rhapsodic prose suggests he enjoyed laying bare our capacity to abuse love and power, and like me in my not so secret thoughts, he savored the blurring of life and fiction. Old desires proved irresistible, and he allowed himself to fondle the past, perhaps intended a little love song to his own childhood sweetheart as he dreamed *Lolita*. In his autobiography *Speak, Memory*, Nabokov writes: "When I first met Tamara—to give her a name concolorous with her real one—she was fifteen, and I was a year older." He remembers the moment he first saw her "in a birch grove," and that he watched her and two other girls "from a vantage point above the river." After that day, he found the cottage where she was living for the summer and began to ride his bicycle or horse nearby with hopes of meeting her, until, on August 9, 1915 at half past four in the afternoon, he finally spoke to her.

The Last Good Obsession

Like love-matched Humbert and Annabel, the real life Nabokov and Tamara sneak away to secret places where they can be alone to taste the delights of romance. So many years later, Nabokov still returns to thoughts of his beloved, as if to a living fantasy: "Seen through the carefully wiped lenses of time, the beauty of her face is as near and as glowing as ever." So many years later, Tamara's frozen-in-time image is brought to life by an aging man, like a fantasy-plagued Humbert shaping Lolita from the Annabel mold.

———

Having brushed against the magic of Nabokov's experiment with vivifying the past, I took my high school yearbook from the bottom shelf of a bookcase in the living room. I knew it was there, having reclaimed it from my childhood home, but I don't remember when I last looked at it. I opened it to the section dedicated to graduating seniors, and a collage of photographs shows twenty young people peering from carefully spaced rectangles. The boys all look uncomfortable wearing suits and neckties and forced smiles. A few of the girls wore pullover sweaters and necklaces for their pictures, while the rest of us posed in an off-the-shoulder, velvet tunic provided by the photographer. Looking perky with my dirty blonde hair cut in a pixie style, I flash a cheerleader smile to match my sparkly eyes. A girl named Lilly, whose photograph is next to mine, wrote something about our senior play on the space between our faces, reminding me of the blue chalk powder that our math teacher/play director (whom I heard had died a few years ago) sprinkled through my hair in an attempt to make me look like the elderly Ethel Savage I was supposed to become for two nights. On the same page, Ramona wrote, "Gosh are you lucky to be getting away to a place where you can really let it all hang out." Other girls quoted love songs of the day, and one mentioned "getting your man"—as if they knew what I pretended not to know. A boy named Greg wrote, "I love your body of water in your swimming pool." The boy I dated off and on through middle school and most of high school didn't write anything.

The supposedly comical "Class Will" claims that the girl I was "leaves her sewing ability to the homemaking class. (It might come in HANDY.)" A photograph in the "Senior Hall of Fame" shows me seated on a folding chair in the school gym wearing a skirt and jacket with a matching sweater (*I remember the green tweed wool of the suit and the scalloped pattern at the neck of the sweater*), black loafers, and stockings. My legs are primly crossed and a boy named Don pretends to be shining my shoes. We look so young (*even though I was pretending to be grown up in that outfit*) and we've just been voted "most likely to succeed" by our classmates.

Teachers were separated into two groups for photographs that appear at the front of the yearbook: One shot shows ten frumpy, sexless women, middle-aged and older, under the heading "Grade Teachers." The other captures the "Junior-Senior High Teachers," and my French teacher sits among them. He looks like a kid, a kid dressed up in a checkered sport coat. The slicked down blonde hair and black-rimmed glasses that I once found so attractive seem nerdy now, so many years later. The scent of desire does not rise from the page, and the emotions I reclaim from this photograph could not fuel a story of obsession. Instead, I could tell you something about imagining and then choosing a path into the world that waited beyond a small town. That's all; nothing else.

But why do I keep returning to the forbidden desires and self-serving deceits of *Lolita,* as if important clues to my own life might nestle in the turn of a pedophilic phrase? And why did I enter my French teacher's name on an internet search to see if I might find where he works or lives, perhaps a photograph of him at some newsworthy event? I would like to watch him without being seen—except for a moment, from a distance, and I would look serene and beautiful just before disappearing as if in a waking dream. Does he ever retrieve the brown vinyl-covered yearbook from some cluttered shelf to look at me? Does he ever wonder whether the girl voted "most likely to succeed" found success?

Who is that girl who looks out from the yearbook photograph above my name? Does desire lead her to "weave her own web," to choreograph the subtle seduction of a man whom she'd transformed in fantasies? Are her pale blue eyes reason enough for him to risk phoning her, or does he love looking at the worldly man he sees reflected in those eyes? She likes the thrill of reaching for what she isn't supposed to have, a "girlish game" with "fluid" rules, and she likes basking in success and feeling alive. Perhaps she needs him until she grows more confident—until she grows increasingly restless and curious and wants to risk more, wants to try on the costume of a "fast little article" for her next act.

The strippers, the pedophiles, Dolores, and me: All of us confounded by the blurring of fantasy and reality in the drama of desire. With my initial fascination out of the way, I returned once more to the burlesque exhibit to ask the strippers about the lure of the forbidden. I found that their photographs tell stories about personas and erotic games, but the shadowy beholders are there as well, begging to be surprised, begging to feel alive.

Pantera Nera—seemingly all about sparkling pasties, fringed panties, and long black gloves—wears a cross necklace that dangles in her cleavage. An athletic little temptress in silky black tap pants and brassiere is frozen mid-air while executing a somersault. A teeny bikini and fishnet might begin one ingénue's outfit, but a mortarboard graduation cap completes her costume. A woman with sultry eyes teases the camera while posing with a look-alike doll, same dress, same hairstyle. Dottie Deane with her primly coiffed hair and tasteful drop earrings got caught with her creamy breasts spilling out of an unbuttoned cardigan sweater. She looks to have just finished the ironing, or a cup of tea, when something unexpected and delightful happened. A plump girl with a large bow pinned in her curls wears a puffy gown with heart cutouts scattered across its full skirt. Decked-out in a sexy brassiere, garter belt, stockings, and hat, Cindy Parker struts her stuff as "The Youngest Star in Burlesque." *How young?*

Then fantasy and reality collide in what may be the most thought-provoking piece in the exhibit. A pretty young woman with sad eyes has inscribed a personal message on her photograph, surely for an admirer. She poses demurely in a long gown, looks a little lonely *(perhaps I'm already imagining a story for her, just as I sometimes shape my own)*, and her words seem aimed at something meaningful and dignified:

> "To Mr. Isenberg a very nice person
> Best Wishes Dolores"

———

Consider this reality: My French teacher probably could not imagine me as I am, forty years after we first met. He might expect, and he'd be right, that my body has grown thicker and my thoughts more complicated, but he couldn't know the particulars of my life. He doesn't know that beneath the deception of a dye named Spiced Cider, my hair is mostly gray. He doesn't know that when I undress, the stretch marks rippling across my hips remind me of those months when I felt perfectly satisfied while waiting for babies—or that two silvery scars remind me of a benign breast tumor one year, and a fiery appendix the next. He is not there to know that now, when I step from bed in the morning, I limp until stiff joints loosen and agree to cooperate. Nor does he know that as I move through the day, worries about my children *(are they safe, are they happy, does their work fulfill them)* slip in and out of my consciousness. He might imagine me still a nurse, unaware that my days are now spent touching and turning ideas as I read and write and remember.

She sinks into the pillows propped against the headboard of her single bed and begins shaping French vocabulary words with her lips. She plans tomorrow's special outfit, maybe the short, buttery yellow dress with pearl buttons and lace-trimmed sleeves. She knows she looks good in that, pure innocence—and he'll notice. Conjugate irregular verbs to the music playing beneath her skin, and the half-slip with the wide lace hem that shows when she crosses her legs, je suis, tu es, and the sling-back loafers that make her legs look long, yeah, yeah, yeah. The phone rings and her mouth goes dry after hello. He says just to talk. What now? What now? For a moment, she considers pulling back, stopping what's been set in motion—what she's set in motion. Or did he? She could say her parents don't allow her to talk on the phone for long, but she doesn't, can't, doesn't want to. She can't believe he called her. A little further, a little further to know what's next.

I don't know how long I'll stay away from him, but for now, I'm finished with Humbert's radiant, tortured life, finished with the "bits of marrow sticking to it, and blood, and beautiful bright-green flies." Once upon a time, he "schemed and dreamed—and the red sun of desire and decision (the two things that create a live world) rose higher and higher. . . ." But always in the end, he finds that his fantasy-driven obsession with Lolita destroys them both. Floating on the currents of Humbert's desire and failure, I've remembered the sometimes-joy of sometimes winning "the race between my fancy and nature's reality," as sometimes happens. But enough—for now.

Advancing the Plot

"You must *act*, my dear; in your situation
the great thing is to act,". . . .
—Henry James, *Washington Square*

The silky loops that fit over fabric knots to join the front halves of my new white blouse weren't working as intended. When I moved my arms and shoulders certain ways, two or three of those closures might slip open at once. I'd glance down to discover that I was flashing cleavage and lace, sometimes with a clear view all the way down to a freckled midriff. My fingers worked to plump the knots larger and twist the loops smaller. Each fix lasted for a promising, modest interval, only to be undone by some activity like riffling through my purse. *Why don't I carry a few pins? Why didn't this happen before I left the apartment?*

All this happened in Manhattan where I wasn't working as intended—and I hadn't been for the past five days. Sitting beside a desk in a writers' workspace called Paragraph, I tried to send a few ideas about Henry James and me onto the computer screen, and I also tried to think about what I would talk about that evening when I joined the editor and staff of a respected literary journal at a dive called Mo Pitkin's House of Satisfaction for readings by two up-and-coming writers from Brooklyn. But I couldn't concentrate; I was worried about where to buy safety pins.

Sandra Swinburne

The day had just begun and I already needed discipline: I would hold my arms close to my body while I worked, and only stray from my alcove if absolutely necessary. I'd wear my coat when I left at four-thirty, no matter how warm the weather, and find a store that sells pins before boarding the train for the Lower East Side. But first, I'd e-mail my friends at home with an update on my writing life: "I haven't bumped into Joan Didion or Jon Stewart yet, but listen to this: I'm actually going out tonight and my blouse. . . ."

I had come to New York looking for adventure, because I'd noticed that my daring was once again missing, that I was fading—that I was boring. Another long winter in upstate New York had made me feel like a ghost in a ghost town; icy morning after icy morning had found me at a kitchen window, drinking coffee and looking out on a quiet, tree-lined street. *I can stay in my pajamas all day long if I want. I might not see another living soul for the next twelve hours, until my husband returns from the hospital around seven.* There I was, living the good life—kids grown and scattered around the country, food in the fridge, gas in the car, unemployed but for trying to write a book—and feeling alternately flat or anxious. On the day when these perceptions came together, I could have walked the dog or combed the cat's matted fur and then faced my computer screen. Instead, I cooked up a plan to borrow my youngest son's Brooklyn apartment for fifteen days during late April and early May (he was at his girlfriend's most of the time anyway), and buy a one-month membership at a writer's room.

This whole brainstorm scared me, and that's what I wanted, what I *needed.* I had visited New York three or four times as a tourist, but never alone; my husband or adult children had steered me around town during each of those trips. With the "alone" part added, I plunged into scene-making like a fiction writer: Crowds of strangers milled around me, none smiling, none talking, and none bothering to care about the others. I glimpsed the sinister form of a murderer or a rapist or a thief lurking in the shadows of an alley. I watched yellow cabs speed past with the faces of frightened women pressed against back windows. I could make myself shiver.

I remembered accounts of New York life that ought to serve as cautionary tales, like Stephen Crane's *Maggie: A Girl of the Streets*. Now there's a sad story about how a woman can be preyed upon, how a city can simply swallow her up whole (never mind that poverty and ignorance determined Maggie's doom at birth). What about the drug-addled despair in *Bright Lights, Big City*, Jay McInerney's look at modern Manhattan's fast lane? And the money-mad hedonism of Don DeLillo's *Cosmopolis*? Wasn't the wrong place at the wrong time a catalyst for disaster in Tom Wolfe's *Bonfire of the Vanities*? With my usual tilt toward disaster, I weighed the challenges of making my own way in that city, reasoning that if I had to, *really had to*, I could call my son or his roommate for help.

Scanning internet book blurbs for a New York classic that would feed my imagination differently from the novels I'd already read, I settled on Henry James' *Washington Square*. Sure enough, the old city's "established repose" charmed me, the inhumanity of Doctor Austin Sloper appalled me, and the female characters provided clues about the baffling enigma of my own self. At first, I felt worried and sympathetic about young Catherine Sloper's passive nature, but then I grew angry as she repeatedly fails to resist those who manipulate the course of her life. I preferred allegiance to Mrs. Lavinia Penniman, the busybody aunt who loves being in the midst of drama, and schemes to set events in motion—even though Catherine's life is her primary project. *After all, am I not trying to make something happen as I test self-discovery and self-determination in my own life?*

I tried to like Catherine because the poor little rich girl needs a champion—any champion. The esteemed Dr. Sloper considers her a sorry substitute for his first born, a son who died at age three, and a sad reminder of his beloved wife who died after giving birth to her. When Catherine is ten years old, he enlists his widowed sister Lavinia to come live with them, and two years later, he gives these instructions: "'Try and make a clever woman of her, Lavinia; I should like her to be a clever woman.'" But Doctor Sloper readily resigns all pretense of hope, believing that his daughter is destined to be obedient and dull.

When Catherine reaches marriageable age without any likely prospects, her father is not a bit surprised; he sees her as robust and plain with a "lively taste for dress" that does not suit her. But on the occasion of her cousin's engagement party, the handsome Morris Townsend lavishes attention on this naive young woman and makes her feel giddy: "Catherine had never heard anyone—especially any young man—talk just like that. It was the way a young man might talk in a novel. . . ." Doctor Sloper, in the habit of indulging both irony and cruelty when dealing with his daughter, credits her "'opulent'" red gown for having attracted a fortune hunter's attention: "'You look as if you had eighty thousand a year.'"

Morris extends his charm to Mrs. Penniman by "saying clever things" that delight her and inquiring about Catherine. During the carriage ride home, Lavinia chatters about the evening and about Catherine's admirer, but Doctor Sloper focuses on the gown's message. In a rare moment of guile, Catherine refuses to admit that she knows the young man's name. And Lavinia, owing to her love of intrigue, fails to mention that she encouraged him to call at their Washington Square residence in the near future.

Widowed after ten years of marriage to a Poughkeepsie minister, Lavinia relies on an irrepressible imagination to "thicken the plot" and make things interesting. She admits that she is not brave, and her brother accuses her of having little common sense, but she steadily refuses to be discouraged from the pleasures of an imaginative life:

She was romantic; she was sentimental; she had a passion for little secrets and mysteries—a very innocent passion, for her secrets had hitherto always been as unpractical as addled eggs. She was not absolutely veracious; but this defect was of no great consequence, for she had never had anything to conceal. She would have liked to have a lover, and to correspond with him under an assumed name, in letters left at a shop. I am bound to say that her imagination never carried the intimacy further than this.

When the possibility of a relationship between Catherine and Morris surfaces, Lavinia seizes the opportunity to transfer her own pent-up energies into a creative act. With neither husband nor child of her own, Lavinia hopes to transform her niece's lackluster existence into the stuff of romance novels, and she anticipates basking in vicarious delight as she watches a courtship develop between a steady young woman and a beautiful young man. To Lavinia, the match seems ideal, and she "even took for granted at times that other people had as much imagination as herself. . . ."

I had arrived at Skillman Avenue in Brooklyn hoping to "'make a clever woman'" of myself, but I soon wanted Mrs. Penniman with her unflinching imagination and penchant for intrigue as my companion. My son Alec and his roommate Dave insisted that their neighborhood was safe enough—except for a murder last summer, probably connected to drug dealers—and they didn't even notice anymore that their landlord runs a construction company from an aluminum trailer parked amidst monster trucks in the lot next to their apartment. That metal and dirt empire is surrounded by chain link fence standing fifteen feet high, with broad gates secured by heavy locks. (Lavinia and

I had some suspicions about the kind of business that really goes on behind those gates.)

Inside the apartment, I scanned the recently tidied rooms, still cluttered, still dusty, but bohemian and thrilling to me. My bulky suitcase fit into a clearing on Alec's bedroom floor, and I decided to simply live out of it for the coming weeks rather than unpack and find hangers. Scratching my ankles, I tried not to think about the bed-bug problem that had raged through the apartment just eight months before. *The place was fumigated; my arms and legs can't really itch.* I filled the freezer with cookies and brownies I'd brought from home, and scanned the moldy ruins within the refrigerator. As a way of "paying" rent and contributing to my own comfort, I cleaned the kitchen and bathroom. Possibilities for the days ahead bubbled through my mind while I scraped mold and scoured porcelain; happily off-balance, I imagined myself starring in a variety of fictions.

My next job was to study a map of the L train route that burrows beneath Brooklyn and Manhattan. I reasoned that a scouting trip to find the closest station at Graham Avenue and a grocery store for toilet paper would give me practice for my actual commutes. But waves of anxiety blurred my thinking when I left the apartment and began trying to memorize markers: *Basketball court at the corner, flowers under an awning, bagel shop over here, another over there.* The five-block neighborhood between the construction lot and the subway stop was a crazy mix of no-frills residential buildings and no-frills retail space. A lot of real people were packed into small spaces, which meant that there was no shortage of shops selling toilet paper.

When I spotted a Graham Avenue sign at stairs leading underground, I went down to see where and how I would begin my travels each day. I watched people insert their tickets at the turnstiles, and made sure that I knew where to wait for Manhattan-bound trains. But when I saw the touch-screen machine that I had to tackle in order to buy a ticket, a surge of panic hit: *Read; just read and respond. Start, in English, regular Metrocard, pay cash, ten dollars, no receipt, thank you.* The "unlimited rides" purchase option confused me, but I'd investigate that later. I had a ticket in my pocket.

At six-thirty the next morning, I heard the rumble of truck engines and the beep, beep, beep warning of big vehicles moving backwards. *Two weeks of waking up to this.* The borrowed bed with a pronounced pitch to one side had been urging me to roll off all night, so I gave in and went to the kitchen to make coffee in a grungy four-cup pot. Dave's door was shut, which meant that he must have come home last night, so I tried not to make any noise. While the pot hissed water over grounds, I looked out the living room window at rooftops and empty alleys. The buildings looked dead; probably everyone else in the neighborhood was used to the truck noises. After the coffee maker's last sputter, I filled a mug and returned to bed where I curled under the covers, re-reading *Washington Square* until I could convince myself that I was ready—Lavinia "suddenly appeared, one morning, with pink roses in her cap"—to negotiate the streets, the stairs, and the inbound L train.

Alone among strangers, enveloped by tunnel and train, the clanging of metal against metal and the squeaks and jolts: All of that drove my pulse. *What happens when a subway train breaks down between stations— under a river? Are there tow trains? What if I actually see one of those unattended bags mentioned in the warning signs? At least five people look suspicious to me. What if there's a break in the tunnel and water comes flooding in? What if. . . .* I was relieved to get off at Union Square and relieved to see a sign for Fifth Avenue. Setting out to find Paragraph on Fourteenth Street near Sixth, where I had an appointment to register and pay, I simultaneously walked and gawked until a Fourth Avenue sign let me know that I was headed the wrong way. A longer hike in the opposite direction ended at a doorway next to a lamp-and-fixture display window belonging to Lighting and Beyond. The black door belonging to Paragraph was propped open with a brick, but being two hours early, I decided that I shouldn't go up yet. Instead, I'd backtrack and explore a few retail opportunities—which, to me, means shoe stores.

Sling-backs and slides shuffled through my head as I rode an escalator up one floor to a DSW store. But I hadn't looked through even two aisles when alarm blasts began, complete with flashing red lights above the exits. I reoriented myself, fixed my radar on the door nearest the escalator, and made my move to leave—but everyone else kept shopping. Could that noise be anything but a fire alarm? Why did dozens of women continue to fondle shoes and gab about what was in style and what was a good deal? Go? Stay? I wanted to stay, but I couldn't stand the uncertainty. I took the exit and rode the escalator to street level where I watched new shoppers walk beneath a blasting, flashing red signal, and step onto the moving ridges that would deliver them deeper into the building. A police car and fire company vehicle arrived, but none of the occupants seemed concerned. *Do they do things differently in New York?* I went to a coffee shop and read until it was time for my meeting.

———

The belated discovery that Morris has been calling at Washington Square provokes Doctor Sloper to strike with thinly disguised cruelty. As a way of belittling the visits *and* his daughter, he asks her if there has been a proposal of marriage, then sets out to investigate Morris' background, convinced that he is not a true gentleman. Morris gauges the enemy and suggests that Catherine might speak to her father in his defense, but she refuses to risk such a conversation, explaining, "'I never contradict him.'" Instead, she remains silent about Morris' attention, even though it is "the most important, the most absorbing thing in her life." Determined to end the covert romance advancing under his own roof, Doctor Sloper confronts Lavinia, whose inspirations foster the affair.

Mrs. Penniman walks a smart line to preserve her domestic security within her brother's patriarchal realm. For a time, she finds that "tasting of the sweets of concealment" with regard to Catherine and Morris may be her best tactic. Wily when pressed by her brother

The Last Good Obsession

for information about occurrences in the house, she feigns ignorance: "'I believe that last night the old gray cat had kittens.'" Yet once the brother/sister duel for power begins in earnest, Lavinia makes a point of claiming lofty motivations—"'I am incapable of betraying a confidence'"—and asserts that her interest in Morris is sympathy-based, since "'he is so interesting'" due to "'misfortunes.'" Her observation that Catherine is happy should (but ironically does not) move Doctor Sloper toward fatherly connection with his daughter; instead, he infers that Catherine is "'a weak-minded woman with a large fortune.'" Sloper insists on reason ruling the day, while Lavinia, hoping to create something romantic and fine, refuses to budge from the side of imagination. In an act of feminist courage, she strikes out at her brother, informing him that he is dead wrong in his underestimation of Catherine, and walks "majestically away."

———

Registered and in possession of Paragraph's official rules, keys, and codes, my first day on the job was a sunny and hot Sunday. I packed a case with laptop, books, and papers, and launched my commute which, having survived it the day before, already seemed less threatening. I disembarked, strode through the station, re-entered the bright world, and walked right up to the familiar black door that was now locked. Taking the key from my pocket, I slid it into the lock and it wouldn't turn. Pull, push, twist, again, and again, and the key didn't work. Sweating and a little shaky, I clutched my purse against my body and shifted the heavy computer bag to the other shoulder while strangers stopped next to me to look at the wares offered by Lighting and Beyond. *A purse snatcher. A drifter hoping to slip into the building when I open the door; he'll pretend he forgot his own key. He'll hide in the loft. Steal food from the members' fridge. Mug some middle-of-the-night writer who's slumped over his keyboard or passed out on the couch. Well, nobody's getting in with this key.* I tried one more time and gave up.

Walking toward the subway entrance, I decided to go to the apartment, change into comfortable clothes, and find a park. But then I realized I was glad the key didn't work. I was afraid to sit in that room full of alcoves and desks and writing writers and find that I had nothing to tap out on my keyboard. My head had begun to ache; I wanted to go back to Brooklyn—so I shouldn't. Returning to the door, I *lifted* the knob while twisting the key and heard a *click*.

———

Catherine's docile approach to womanhood—knowing neither how to flirt nor fight and not caring to learn—becomes steadily more frustrating. Morris says that he cannot enter the house after her father "'taunted'" his poverty, and asks her to meet him in Washington Square. But Catherine is without daring and without curiosity, so she insists that they meet within the familiar propriety of the parlor during her father's absence. On hearing Morris' report of this, Lavinia can scarcely believe that a woman could resist "a sentimental tryst beside a fountain sheeted with dead leaves," and marvels over the "oddity—almost the perversity—of the choice."

Lavinia finds Morris irresistible and thinks: "'That's the sort of husband I should have had!'" She sees in him the sort of worldly man with whom her fantasies might have been made manifest, yet insists that her concerns for his happiness mirror those felt by a mother or sister. When Morris no longer calls at the house after being intimidated by Doctor Sloper's resolution to be rid of him, Lavinia writes him every day to make up for her niece's failure to nurture the romantic plot, but more than that, she writes because she wants to.

Eager to stake out her own starring role in the fanciful scenarios she envisions, Lavinia plans a clandestine meeting with Morris and considers Greenwood Cemetery or the Battery. She finally settles on a "tryst at dusk" in "an oyster saloon in the Seventh Avenue, kept by a Negro." Setting her plan in motion, she goes to the rendezvous "enveloped in an impenetrable veil," and talks with Morris in "the duskiest corner of the back shop." She drinks tea while her companion eats oyster stew, "and it is hardly too much to say that this was the happiest half hour that Mrs. Penniman had known for years."

———

Three days of sitting in a cubicle at Paragraph with a candy bowl calling my name. I shut the lid on my laptop, pushed away from the desk, tiptoed through the silent aisles, opened and closed the door as if to a nursery (or a sick room), and filled my lungs with air from the outside world. Besides, it was late afternoon and I needed to check for cell phone messages; perhaps my son and his girlfriend wanted to meet me for dinner. I went into the lounge, filled a mug with water, got out my phone, and positioned myself at the table where candy and the *New York Times* waited. After glancing around corners to see that nobody was in the office or bathroom, I began mainlining Tootsie Rolls, disposing of each little piece of waxed-wrapper-evidence as soon as I peeled it off. Then I switched to caramels. *Maybe I'll read the Times for just a little while. I wish I'd eaten lunch. Maybe a field trip to Washington Square would put me in writing mode. I feel sick.*

So far, the e-mails between my friends and me were more interesting than anything else I'd written. They received a full report about the near disaster at the apartment when I put a bagel in the toaster and left the room to get dressed—only to smell smoke, run back, and find flames shooting out of the slots where the too-thick pieces were wedged. My relief at pulling the plug and sliding the toaster into the sink before the cupboards caught fire became their relief as well. I regaled them with a description of me weighted down by a large purse, computer case, and grocery bags ("Big mistake to buy milk and juice.") while standing braced against a pole on the crowded commuter train that rocked and rolled back to Brooklyn. I wanted them to really *see* me hauling that load up the subway steps, trudging past gangs of kids, skirting the construction lot, and then struggling not to fall backwards on the last flight of stairs into the second floor apartment. Jean had cheered me on, urging me to be brave, and Jim had begun calling me "Little Nell."

I slipped a few Tootsie Rolls in my pocket and returned to the quiet room to pack up: I was going to Washington Square. With map in hand, I set out to find where the house belonging to Henry James' grandmother had once stood. Internet research informed me that the model for Doctor Sloper's "wide-fronted house, with a big balcony" had once occupied Number 18 Washington Square North; I arrived at the address to find a parking garage connected to a brick apartment building in its place. Several other Greek revival houses remain, and I walked back and forth in front of them, trying and failing to detect "the strange odor of the ailanthus trees" which James describes. With banners and an admission office sign posted above Number 22, New York University appears to have infiltrated the area's "established repose."

I crossed into the park where I sat on a bench, imagined the vanished house, and listened to jazz being played on a battered alto sax by a young man down the walk. The steady back beat of traffic mixed his sad notes with the happy squeals of children running inside the fenced playground opposite the apartments. Daffodils and grape hyacinths popped up beside the pavement. A woman sat next to me wearing a very short dress with fishnet stockings and high black boots. I tried to picture a small boy of long ago dawdling in the park, or perhaps sulking on the front steps. I caught a whiff of cigarette smoke in the air, wished it were mine, and gathered my bags for the walk back to the subway.

A few days later (with little writing progress made), I stepped out from the station at Union Square and the weather was brilliant, more like summer than spring, and an outdoor market had popped up overnight. Buckets of flowers, baskets of fruits and vegetables and artisanal breads: I couldn't sentence myself to an air-conditioned alcove;

The Last Good Obsession

I wanted to browse. Who would suspect that plastic bags full of dirt were sold as fixings for earthworm condominiums? (Think composting.) I nearly bought the faux vintage poster of a nuzzling couple beneath the caption "Martinis, lowering standards since 1928," but couldn't think where I'd put it. A sidewalk artist crawled along the edges of a chalky landscape adding more darkness to an already foreboding scene. *How does he cope with knowing that, as soon as he leaves, countless sneakers and sandals will trample his gray and purple sky?*

When I'd had enough of the crowded marketplace, I persuaded myself (with perhaps the same inclination that makes me a re-reader of books) that I could think differently about writing with a return visit to Washington Square. I walked down Fifth Avenue and dallied at the intersection of Ninth Street to eavesdrop on a smartly dressed old lady telling a smartly dressed middle-aged man that he certainly had caused the collision of their cars: "And you know that is the truth as well as I do," she said. With a flourish of her hand, she directed his attention to the creased metal along the passenger side of her silver BMW. He did not even attempt to argue.

Nearing the square, I noticed police officers standing in clusters, and then police cars and vans parked along the side streets. I heard a man's amplified voice that sounded excited, but couldn't understand what he was saying until he shouted, "Burn all the books and start history over again!" Inside the park, two young women continued tossing a football, assorted couples continued walking and holding hands, and nobody seemed particularly surprised by the verbal directive. I didn't know what to think other than Little Nell was surely getting around town, and this day was too good to be true.

I walked toward a rigged speaker's platform near the fountain where a red and white banner proclaimed: "CURES NOT WARS." A gray-haired man holding a microphone stood center stage and rambled on about supposed biblical references to the use of cannabis: "Bless this demonstration for this honored herb. This honored herb will bring a better mind with which to commune with the best mind." I figured I was an unsuspecting member of a demonstration in support of legalizing marijuana, and imagined my children laughing about me being mistaken for a pothead.

Then the weird-o-meter really rocketed when the pot priest called into the crowd: "I need volunteers to participate in a Homeric sacrifice. Some of you step right up here." A frizzy-haired young man bounced onto the platform—obviously not worried about the word *sacrifice*—and then, out of nowhere, a lumpy, not-young woman materialized next to him. I cringed with the recognition that she was wearing nothing but a nude-colored brassiere on her top half, and that her sagging breasts drooped onto a sagging midriff which drooped over the elastic waist of black slacks. I was embarrassed for her, but looking around, all signs suggested that she was okay in this crowd. Meanwhile, the mumbo jumbo continued as the celebrant poured what he claimed was lettuce juice into paper cups, warned the volunteers not to drink until after he offered prayer, and then droned incantations.

I had gravitated to a watcher's seat on a low, cement wall. Across from me, a disheveled woman clapped her hands and offered a few weak rounds of chanting, while next to her a slim middle-aged man with curly hair and a full beard applied lipstick. His long, fuchsia-lacquered fingernails and the bead bracelets on each wrist suggested a love for pretty things, as did his chartreuse chiffon blouse, metallic gold belt, and lavender clogs. Draped at his side lay a fake-fur jacket, but for now, in the heat of the day, his sunglasses and white straw hat were simply perfect as he tilted his head to light a cigarette and blow smoke from the corner of his glistening lips.

The next speaker explained that the thirty-fifth annual pot parade would begin shortly, and organizers were so happy to be back in Washington Square Park, having endured a brief relocation after being banned from the Square in 1997. I'd had enough of the pot party, but I couldn't wait to tell my family and friends about what I'd seen and heard in the park.

The Last Good Obsession

I crossed the grass to a bench opposite the phantom Number 18 and tried to wonder about Henry James: What would he make of the varied states of dress and undress in today's Square? What would he think about individual experience of gender and sexuality being expressed in public? Earlier in the week, a few clicks through the internet had taken me to a statement credited to Faulkner in which he calls James "the nicest old lady I ever met." My response had been immediate: *I don't ever want to be anyone's nicest old lady.* Perhaps that reading of James the man explains why James the author does not seduce me the way Faulkner and others do. He allows Catherine no more than an occasional chaste kiss, and his tight control over desire hovers like a scolding. Catherine and Lavinia, one draped in heavy gowns, the other cloaked in adorned widow's weeds, are never allowed to actually *live* in physical bodies. Sitting where James once surely walked, I don't even crave his company. *I want to feel precipitous life, not coldness and obedience.*

———

Doctor Sloper informs Catherine that he will disinherit her if she chooses to marry Morris, certain that her suitor will experience a change of heart after hearing this news. He follows up the next day by advising Lavinia of his intentions, warning her that he will consider further encouragement of the romance an act of treason. When he claims authority over Catherine's well-being based on his expertise as a physician, Lavinia steels herself to respond: "'Your being a distinguished physician has not prevented you from already losing *two members* of your family.'"

Catherine assures Morris that she intends to marry him, and her father's disinheritance will not result in their financial ruin since she receives money from her mother's estate. Catherine's refusal to give up the forbidden romance motivates Doctor Sloper to plan a father/daughter trip to Europe, believing that a prolonged separation will cause Morris to seek the comforts he desires with some other woman of means.

Lavinia decides that there is need for caution in the romantic scheme, and contacts Morris to advise a delay of marriage plans. He accuses her of thinking more than necessary, to which she replies: "'I suppose I do; but I can't help it, my mind is so terribly active. When I give myself, I give myself. I pay the penalty in my headaches, my famous headaches—a perfect circlet of pain! But I carry it as a queen carries her crown.'"

With the Slopers in Europe, Lavinia takes quick possession of the newly lively house and the new freedom to entertain Morris. She invites him to tea and allows him to sit in her brother's private study, later telling Catherine: "'I may almost say *I* have lived with him.'" *Lavinia! This was your chance. Why didn't you break free of Mr. James and his careful plot? All sorts of things might have happened if only you'd trusted yourself to visit other oyster saloons and walk through the park on dusky evenings, with Morris or by yourself. Who cares what Mr. James expects or allows? Who cares what people think? Other female characters overwhelm their authors; Joanna Burden and Oedipa Maas make demands, and their creators are taken aback by the femaleness of their needs. You could have, Lavinia; you could have advanced your own plot.*

Catherine is ready to marry Morris, and willing to accept her father's displeasure and a reduced inheritance. However, her suitor had counted on Dr. Sloper changing his mind about their marriage. Wanting to extricate himself from the relationship, Morris tells Catherine that there is talk about him marrying for money, so he must leave to earn his own way; he promises that they will meet again, and later sends her a letter in which he expresses hope that they can remain friends. Catherine settles on never risking her heart again, and "before she was forty she was regarded as an old-fashioned person and an authority on customs that had passed away." But before her father's death, she finds the courage to refuse his final request for a promise that she will never marry Morris Townsend: "She knew herself that she was obstinate, and it gave her a certain joy. She was now a middle-aged woman."

While Catherine sinks into a quiet, prideful life within the house on Washington Square, Mrs. Penniman appears "quite a girlish figure; she grew younger as she advanced in life. She lost none of her relish for beauty and mystery, but she had little opportunity to exercise it." On a particularly balmy July evening, she sits "forward in the window, half on the balcony, humming a little song" as she prepares to inform Catherine, who sits "within the room, in a low rocking chair, dressed in white," of her latest secret.

⸻

On the day of the faulty blouse, at exactly four-thirty, I packed my writing gear into a red nylon carrying case. But more importantly, I put on my gray twill coat, refastened the knots and loops that had come undone during this flurry of activity, and left Paragraph in search of safety pins. I thought about asking a salesgirl in a clothing store if there were any pins tossed in a drawer, but the shops on this stretch of Fourteenth looked trendy and youthful, unlikely to have a stash of fix-it supplies. When I came to a drugstore with room fans, toys, and other miscellany in the front window, I figured I was set; I left with a box of forty safety pins in my pocket and a belief that my worries were nearly over.

The route to Mo Pitkin's that I'd printed from the internet seemed doable, even for someone as direction-impaired as me. I found the platform for the F train going toward Coney Island *(Coney Island?)*, hopped aboard the next train, and counted the stops until reaching Second Avenue. *Exit and find East Houston, walk east to Avenue A, turn left. I can do this in the daylight—but a few hours from now and I'll have to do it in reverse, plus connect to an L train, plus walk the stretch to the apartment, in the dark.* The evening was warm, too warm to be wearing a coat, so I unbuttoned it, keeping a close eye on the blouse, on my purse, and on my computer case while I walked down the sidewalk.

My plan was to make a beeline for the ladies' room as soon as I got to Mo's, but I walked in and nearly stumbled over the group I was meeting, only one of whom I actually knew. *Exchange names, shake hands, what are you drinking, no, no, I'll get something, where's the bartender, a Stella, please.* I was thrown off by finding them too soon and having to choose what to drink. Then I glanced down to see the familiar expanse of cleavage and lace. Standing at the bar with the man who had invited me to the reading, I fastened a button on my coat while casually mentioning that I needed to wash my hands after traveling by subway and bolted toward the promise of privacy.

In the unisex bathroom, I locked the door, tore off my coat, and began fumbling with the pin box. Starting at the bottom, I pinned each closure from the underside, deciding midway that I'd secured enough territory; the top ones could slip now and then with no harm done. Upstairs, I drank beer, ordered something fried from the menu, and engaged in conversations about reading and writing and New York City. A woman sitting across from me was from Georgia and had been shopping for gifts to take home to her teenaged daughter. A woman named Kathleen with beautiful, dark blonde Caribbean-style braids arrived just before the readings began, and I leaned over to say, "I love your hair; I want it."

The authors read from their work, and each had written about a man tormented by his own thoughts—one piece fiction, the other nonfiction, and both seemed true to me. The fictional man experiences depression and commits suicide; the real man named Russell shuffles religious beliefs, anxiety, suicide fixation, sexual obsession, and drug addiction—turning to pornographic cartoons as a means of expressing his interior life. Some listeners snickered over the X-rated material and I wondered if my own fears about the mind's intricate fragility explained why I couldn't, why Russell's story filled me with sadness.

The Last Good Obsession

Earlier in the evening, a woman had told me how much she liked my blouse and I had told her that I could never pass through a metal detector wearing it. Explanation had followed, I'd laughed and she'd laughed; but having watched her laugh again when she heard about Russell's dirty secrets, I stopped liking her. People milled around and I talked to the woman with braids, asking where she had them done. But I began to worry about the trip back to Brooklyn, so I thanked the people hosting the event, paid my share of the tab, and headed out.

I had never walked the five blocks between the Graham Avenue stop and the apartment alone and after dark, but that night I had no choice. Anticipation of the shadowy alleys between me and safety put me on edge, made me feel ready to run and ready to scream. By the time I turned down Skillman Avenue, I was obsessed with looking for lights in apartment houses, someone retrieving something from a parked car, someone taking out garbage, another woman walking home. Instead of those reassurances, I heard a man singing rap behind me, and his voice seemed to grow closer. (Lavinia and I know that one must get steely at such times: "'Ah, you must not be afraid. Be afraid of nothing, and everything will go well.'") Straightening my shoulders and tightening my pace to create an illusion of confidence, I reviewed where I'd put the key to the apartment and slid my hand into my purse to feel its shape. *March right past the fenced lot, up the front steps, plug the key into the lock, pull the door open, and slam it shut.*

The apartment was stuffy from having been closed all day. I unloaded my bags and opened the window in the corner of the living room, noticing that Dave had left a nearly flat cigarette pack on the sill. But there was at least one—I'd put a dollar bill into the cellophane as an apology—so, slipping off my shoes, I settled into the stained pink chair, turned off the lamp, and groped for the pack and matches. Under the dizzy buzz of sworn-off nicotine, I stared over rooftops into a sky that might have been gray and purple and wondered what I was doing in Brooklyn on this night, and why tomorrow night I would go to dinner and a play, and the next night I would go to readings at

Sandra Swinburne

Columbia, and each night I'd make my way past the construction lot in the dark, alone and frightened.

Poor Catherine, poor Lavinia. So little heat and so little laughter. Were they simply doomed from the start to forever want what James couldn't give them? Catherine gives up, allows the house on Washington Square to devour her—not unlike Crane's poor defeated Maggie surrenders to the jaws of the dark city. Lavinia shows flickers of life, but the careful knot of her creator's plan keeps her in check, keeps her suspended in "almost." And what does Little Nell want? Can she be satisfied with loosening her hair from its pins and sitting "half on the balcony"? Or does she need the rumble of oncoming trains—anything less feeling like failure of nerve? What does she want?

Miracles and Luck

"People don't demand that a thing be reasonable if their emotions
are touched. Lovers aren't reasonable, are they?"
—Graham Greene, *The End of the Affair*

After my third reading of Graham Greene's novel *The End of the Affair*, I still want Sarah Miles to break her promise, but I understand why she can't, as I have since the first: Superstition and fear muddle her thoughts and she can't risk altering the vow she made to a God she doesn't think she believes in—just in case he does exist. I prefer Sarah before she becomes *good*, when she's still physically available yet mysteriously elusive in her relationships. I want to watch how that Sarah listens to her body and plays with danger, carefully slipping in and out of others' lives while pursuing desire. *I think I'll just go on wanting her to toss the vow aside in favor of ordinary happiness.*

Sarah Miles and Maurice Bendrix, the writer with whom she's having an affair, are making love in his London apartment on June 16, 1944 when the wail of sirens announces incoming German bombs. The sound of breaking glass sends Maurice downstairs to investigate, and another explosion leaves him unconscious with the front door resting on top of him. Sarah later records in her diary that she hurried to his side where she was unable to rouse him and could not move the door. Believing him dead, she returned to the bedroom, fell on her knees, and proposed a deal:

Dear God, I said—why dear, why dear?—make me believe. I can't believe. I can't believe. Make me. I said, I am a bitch and a fake and I hate myself. I can't do anything of myself. *Make* me believe. I shut my eyes tight, and I pressed my nails into the palms of my hands until I could feel nothing but the pain, and I said, I will believe. . . . Let him be alive, and I *will* believe. . . . But that wasn't enough. It doesn't hurt to believe. So I said, I love him and I'll do anything if you'll make him alive. I said very slowly, I'll give him up forever, only let him be alive with a chance, and I pressed and pressed and I could feel the skin break. . . .

Sarah tells of having sealed her bargain with this pale stigmata—but then Maurice appeared at the door, "and he was alive, and I thought now the agony of being without him starts, and I wished he was safely back dead again under the door."

———

Twenty-five years ago, the phone rang and I heard that my father had suffered a massive stroke during the night. A flurry of calls between doctors and family resulted in a consensus that specialists and high-tech care were his best chance for recovery, so he was transferred that morning from the small hospital near my old hometown to the sophisticated urban hospital minutes from my present home in Rochester, New York. The sudden gush of unchecked blood within my father's skull had left him unconscious, and the neurologists and neurosurgeons plotted damage control, hoping that his brain could somehow, against the odds, return to some level of normalcy. My mother, sister, and I hovered at Dad's bedside, days passed with no improvement, and our watch continued—each of us in a suspended state that seemed to mirror his own there-but-not-there presence. *Would he wake up, ever again? Please, God, let him get well.*

I went home one afternoon to be with my children for a few hours and to orchestrate whatever necessary to keep disrupted family life limping along. When I returned to my father's room, doctors and nurses crowded around his body in the full clamor of resuscitation efforts. "You should wait outside," a nurse said when she noticed me in the doorway, staring. My father died that night, and I knew I had not prayed hard enough.

Seven and a half years later, the phone rang while I prepared lunch for friends, and once again, everything changed in a moment. My mother's friend Alice told me that Mom had been admitted to the hospital near my hometown with a heart attack, but seemed to be doing okay. After experiencing pain in her left arm and pressure in her chest, Mom had called for the volunteer ambulance; Alice, an Army nurse during World War II, had followed and stayed with her since my mother didn't want to "bother" me until there was a diagnosis. I told Alice that I'd call my sister and we'd get to the hospital as soon as we could. Lunch was cancelled, childcare was arranged, and a plastic grocery bag was packed with a change of clothes and a toothbrush. In less than two hours, my sister and I were driving back to small-town America, and calculating the steps for having Mom transferred to a Rochester hospital as soon as she was stable.

Full of anxiety and doubt as we scanned the minimally equipped intensive care unit, the city daughters reassured Mom that she was doing fine, that she'd be out of there soon, and she looked relieved that we were there to watch and wait. My sister understood the graphs and IV drips and lab reports, having once been a surgical intensive care nurse, so Mom knew that she'd keep an eye on everything that was done. Late that night, when readings and results seemed steady, we two middle-aged women kissed our mother goodnight and drove through black hills, winding through places with names like Birdseye Hollow and Rabbit Road, to the house where we'd been raised.

The house was lifeless without Mom puttering among her things, and my hands shook while I smoked a couple of the cigarettes (even though I'd once again quit) that I'd bought at a gas station near the hospital. I hesitated to enter the guestroom where dead flies speckled the window ledges and stiff twin beds, all done up in electric-blue floral spreads, looked like ugly stepsisters. There was a time when this had been the sickroom where my mother's mother spent the last night of her life, breathing only in sporadic bursts as she lay dying of cancer. There had been a double bed, and a different rocking chair, a wide wicker chair, in which my teenaged self waited while my mother tended my grandmother.

Tucked between stale muslin sheets, my mind lurched between possibilities while my limbs shivered against the dark. *Please, God, take care of her. Let her get well; give me another chance to be a better daughter, to make her happy. Without her, I'd be an orphan—of sorts. A motherless child. Why "child"? At what age will I stop seeking rescue?* Then I made vague promises about doing good deeds and serving those who suffer, if only my mother could live. And she did, but I cannot offer any hard evidence that I kept my end of the bargain. I still get impatient and snappy with her, still only half-listen when she repeats worn-out stories, and still seldom force myself to stay overnight at the house of my childhood, even though I know that would please her. I prefer to drive down, help her into the car with her bags, and drive back to my home where I am comfortable and she is the guest. As for serving others—I only dabble.

An attempt at truth requires adding that those glimpses of threatened loss did not fully test my capacity to request divine intervention; only when I held one and then another of my own children during various illnesses did I know how shards of fear and grief can gouge all reason out of me. Only then did I reveal my full potential to beg and plead and beseech Thee for whatever miracle I wanted and needed. Night after night, stroking a child's temple with my thumb, I have prayed: *Please, God, pour all my will into this small body, through my fingers, send all my strength through my fingers to bring health and happiness to this child. I'll do anything.* I envisioned waves of energy being transfused; I imagined touch healing. I asked God to spare my children and give me suffering instead. My leaps toward hope were magical and relentless, and more than once, a sick child got well. And more than once, maybe soon, or maybe later, my inner world turned to shades of gray. I saw only sadness where others saw the ups and downs of daily life, and I struggled to get out of bed under the weight of feeling depressed. *Perhaps a deal is a deal.*

I wanted to escape the pervading gloom of those payback days that crept through my life; I wanted the ground to stop sinking beneath my feet. Who wouldn't want to weasel out and get something for nothing, if she could? Who wants anyone to know that a desperate bargain with God can come to feel as bitterly binding as Faust's own deal with the devil? Why *wouldn't* Sarah Miles look for a loophole?

After meeting Sarah in 1939, Maurice Bendrix explains that he was attracted to her not only for her beauty, but "because she was happy." He also sees opportunity since he's writing a novel about a civil servant and needs to learn the habits of such a man; Sarah just happens to be married to Henry, "an important assistant secretary in the Ministry of Pensions." But once their love affair begins, calculation and reason fall away: Bendrix finds that he's obsessed with Sarah, and she vows, without a trace of doubt, "'Nobody else. Ever again.'"

One night, after they have sex on the living room floor of the Miles home, Maurice wonders if Sarah minds that her husband is upstairs sick in bed, but she doesn't: "Unlike the rest of us she was unhaunted by guilt. In her view, when a thing was done, it was done: remorse died with the act." Bendrix reports that Sarah "believed in God as little as I did," both having chosen "so happily to eliminate God from our world." But he doesn't know then that Sarah's mother, as a long ago act of revenge against her Jewish husband, took her two-year-old daughter to a Catholic priest for baptism.

Maurice wakens on a June morning and feels that his mind is "a blank sheet on which somebody had just been on the point of writing a message of happiness." Then he discovers that he lies beneath a door that's been blasted from its frame. After freeing himself from the debris, he walks to his bedroom where he finds Sarah crouched on the floor, naked and afraid. She explains that she's praying to "'anything that might exist'" and dresses quickly, pausing only to wash her lover's bloodied face. Before leaving, she tells him she'd thought he was dead—and he teases that she must have prayed for a miracle. But he also recalls Sarah's enigmatic parting words: "'You needn't be so scared. Love doesn't end. Just because we don't see each other. . .'"

———

Churches, one Baptist and one Catholic, stand at opposite ends of the small town where I spent my childhood. However, I never set foot in the Baptist church during those years, believing it was a sin for a good Catholic to trespass there. My Polish immigrant grandparents drove into town from their farm on the hill to attend Holy Day, Lenten, and Sunday services at Saint Stanislaus Roman Catholic Church, a small, white-framed building within sight of our house. And their only daughter, my mother, did her best to make believers of her children, even though church laws of that era banned her from the sacraments for having married my father, an out-of-towner whose previous marriage had ended in divorce.

But until I was around seven years old, when my mother finally told my sister and me that our father had been married before, I didn't understand why she always attended mass, but didn't participate in the sacred rituals. My grandparents periodically entered the dark-curtained confessional with downcast eyes, and I can nearly see my own small face watching my stout grandmother as she seemed to collapse in prayer during the Eucharistic rites, her babushka-wrapped head dropping into her hands while she knelt on the floor. I liked studying the old Polish women who pressed glass rosary beads between their work-thickened fingers while their lips moved through silence. Sometimes they closed their eyes and shaped a fist with which they knocked at their hearts, as if to will an ecstatic breaking and entering, or to plead forgiveness, or perhaps to punish unruly flesh. I listened while their thread-thin voices quavered through hymns in a language that I heard at my grandparents' farm, but didn't understand. Memory gives me moments of hearing those old women, with the church organ groaning behind them, and realizing that every song they sang sounded like a piece of grief primeval that had crossed treacherous seas with them.

I was excited when I was finally among the children collected by Adelaide, the priest's housekeeper, for lessons that would prepare us to receive the sacraments. Standing before us in a stained housedress, the stern and slovenly woman tackled what she surely believed was her holy obligation to teach God's laws. She proclaimed that babies who died without being baptized could not enter the Kingdom of Heaven; that lies, disrespect, and impure thoughts could earn us a spot in hell unless we sought and received absolution; that we must hope non-Catholics would convert for the salvation of their souls; and that failed marriages were a one way ticket out of the fold and into the fire. I recall being scared, but also liking the powerful mystery and demanding rules. However, since my father attended a Methodist church in another town, and my mother never entered the confessional, I tried to imagine how they might be saved—but couldn't.

Until mid-adolescence brought the disruptive forces of doubt and rebellion into my life, I practiced Catholicism with obedience, accepting that rules are rules, as my mother did. I even imagined myself wearing nun's garb, devout and silent. Each week I got out my prayer book with its list of sins, and I examined my conscience for evidence of mortal and venial offences, never figuring out which was which.

Sandra Swinburne

Does missing mass sentence a ten-year-old to hell or only purgatory? What about taking the Lord's name in vain? And what sort of time does one serve for impure thoughts? I took my weekly turn behind the dark curtains and confessed that I was guilty of disrespect, jealousy, lies, and more; but from the very first, I struggled over admission of impure thoughts. Not that I knew for sure just what was meant by that terminology, but it seemed any wondering about bodies must qualify, and a few years of guilt over that already festered within me. *Guilt, guilt, guilt: I'd done nearly everything on the list of sins.*

My practice of Catholicism sputtered toward a finish line during the months before turning eighteen, when I felt ready to test my own powers of reason—and my actual capacity for impure thoughts. I was dating an older guy who was a lapsed Lutheran, and I was leaving town to attend a large university. No more confessions to a shadow-man inside the darkened booth—but the old habit of guilt nagged at me in other darkened rooms and I tried attending mass two or three times during freshman year at college, until, feeling like a bored hypocrite, I stopped. Yet, my guilt doesn't stop, and forty years later, I recognize the Catholic God who harrows the lives of Sarah Miles and Maurice Bendrix.

———

Sarah's confessions in her diary reveal desperate attempts to renege on her promise to give up Maurice: "A vow's not all that important—a vow to somebody I've never known, to somebody I don't really believe in. Nobody will know that I've broken a vow, except me and Him—and He doesn't exist, does he? He can't exist. You can't have a merciful God and this despair." Not that Sarah hasn't finessed her way around the constraints of a promise before: She has remained a loyal companion to her husband for ten years—except for finding excitement in sexual flings, and except for falling in love with Maurice.

But this time, with this vow, she scuffles through reasoning and the knot of her word simply won't be loosed. She's tired of her burden, tired of "pretending to be alive," and imagines giving God an ultimatum: "I can't believe in you, I can't love you, but I've kept my promise. If I don't come alive again, I'm going to be a slut, just a slut. I'm going to destroy myself quite deliberately. Every year I'll be more used. Will you like that any better than if I break my promise?"

Alone and lonely, Sarah walks in the Common hoping to accidentally meet Maurice—if she could just see him without it being her fault—but instead she encounters Richard Smythe, a man with disfiguring facial birthmarks who argues publicly against the existence of God: "I thought, if only he could convince me that you don't have to keep a promise to someone you don't believe in, that miracles don't happen . . . ." Her case for annulment of the vow builds: She was hysterical when she found Maurice under the rubble that last night they were together, perhaps he wasn't dead to her touch, perhaps he wasn't raised by God's hand, and perhaps she's still hysterical. She wants to *know* whether she's stuck with a miracle or merely blind to a fortunate coincidence.

Sarah eventually reaches out to Smythe, hoping to dispatch the promise that lingers "like an ugly vase a friend has given and one waits for a maid to break it, and year after year she breaks the things one values and the ugly vase remains." Smythe, a member of the Rationalist Society, states his mission: "To sting people into thinking for themselves." Sarah tells him she's not a practicing Christian and doesn't want to believe in God, although she "'may have been christened—it's a social convention.'" She describes finding Maurice after the explosion and making a deal that seemed to raise him from the dead. Smythe attempts to deliver the reason she seeks: "'Think of the thousands of people all over the world praying now, and their prayers aren't answered.'"

———

Sarah's emotional turmoil over faith raises so many scenes from my own life that I hardly know where to begin. Growing older, becoming more educated and more experienced with problem-solving through reason, my mind usually doubts that the God of my childhood exists at all, and I seldom attend church services unless to please my mother and/or husband. Yet, I admit that after my children were born, I poured water over each tiny forehead and said, "I baptize thee in the name of the Father, the Son, and of the Holy Spirit"—just in case he does exist. Furthermore, when desperate for help, I still slip into the old cadence of prayer as if by reflex. *Please, God. Please, God.*

In my gloomy times, I suspect that everyone has cancer—but some of us don't yet know. Not so for my friend Mary. She knows. Nearly seven years ago she had surgery and radiation to treat a type of breast cancer that the best medical opinions deemed curable. She believed herself well; her family and friends believed her well. Four years later, before the numbing upstate New York winter gave us cause, she complained that her bones hurt and I said, "So do mine." But mine crackled and ached due to minor arthritic changes, while hers sounded a warning that cancer cells had invaded her ribs and liver. By the following January, her doctors acknowledged that this should not have happened based on every characteristic of her first tumor, but it had. Mary forced herself to process what they said, forced herself to research her own case online, forced herself to confront all the little pieces of prediction until she blurted out, "If I die, I'd want my ashes kept in the house. And it would be really nice if they put them in the car for family trips." *I put too much belief in medical science; it was not working. Please, God, take this back to a time when Mary is well.*

But the insistent Now prevails, and Mary simply wants to live. When she worried that her own naturally pale blonde hair might soon begin sticking to the pillow case and filling her brush, we went to the home of a Hasidic woman who, because her religion forbids a woman's hair from showing in public, specializes in wigs. The expert guided us through style catalogues and recommended cuts and colors that are most like Mary's own, but her bossy approach triggered mischief in Mary, who asked to see wigs with style names like The Caroline and The Ashley, even though they looked nothing like her own hair. Wig-lady went upstairs to a room off limits to us, where hundreds of little boxes line the shelves (so she explained), and one by one she brought what looked like a small, dead animal nestled in her hands for our inspection. Mary with a dark brown layered look, Mary with a green-tinged blonde pixie, Mary with a punked-up razor cut. We laughed at some and chose the best, the style most like her own. It looks like a wig.

Not long after that day, radioactive isotopes traveled through Mary's blood so the doctors could evaluate the condition of her heart as they tried to explain why she was so short of breath. Next came tests for blood clots in her legs, more phone calls, and more consultations until, finally, she was told she must learn to inject an anti-coagulant into her midriff each morning. I watched Mary's hands shake while swabbing the skin and pulling the cap off the needle, and listened when she said afterward that the shot had hurt. I watched as Mary was forced to quit her job as a health care consultant and accept the full-time job of cancer patient.

When Mary's husband was out of town during one of her chemo treatments, I went along to the hospital to keep her company. We saw the nurse practitioner who responded to questions with a perky, this-is-only-cancer-and-you-can-manage-it attitude. We saw the doctor who discussed treatment options, and we waited in the lounge for the chemo nurse to call Mary back for the drip, drip, drip of toxic chemicals. With volunteers weaving among the patients to offer drinks and snacks, I began to feel less frightened—until a woman my age walked past pushing a wheelchair that cradled the skeletal body of a boy near in age to my youngest son, but *not* me and *not* my son. *Please, God, give them courage and let him get well. Heal him. And please, God, never allow such suffering to visit me and mine.*

Sometimes feelings of hopelessness nudge my *Please, God* supplications into existence and they manifest as whispers. At others, a jolt of panic shoots through my body and the adrenaline fuels silent screams. *I need help keeping berserk drivers away from my oldest son as he negotiates the freeways around Washington, D. C., I need help keeping my second son whole as he skis recklessly down Vermont mountains, I need help keeping sharks away from my daughter as she swims through Pacific kelp forests, and I need help keeping airplanes in the sky as my youngest son flies to far off places in search of adventure.* But just who is this God that I run to?

Searching for insight into my own erratic reliance on a patchwork of prayer, I looked under "miracles" in Bartlett's *Familiar Quotations* and found a passage from Turgenev's *Prayer*: "Whatever a man prays for, he prays for a miracle. Every prayer reduces itself to this: 'Great God, grant that twice two be not four.'" *If twice two equals a deadly four, grant that it not be so. Keep them safe. Please, God.* Prayer as white noise: I can run the word sequence through the whole day, like placing an order and repeating it over and over to be sure the server heard it correctly. I can keep it going while I shop for groceries or iron shirts or stare into the dark, sleepless with worry. For emergency intervention, or as a safety net. An insurance policy, just in case. Can't hurt. Simple, really.

Shameless, really. Looking for help from a God to whom I pay little homage. Sometimes, after asking the almighty parent to step in, I imagine a voice without a face remarking to the cherubim and seraphim, "I only hear from her when she wants something." But that doesn't change my needing help—and when a crisis subsides, I try to remember a "thank you."

———

Richard Smythe wants Sarah to see that people create stories to find meaning in their lives, and God is but one more story: "'Man made God in his own image, so it's natural he should love him. You know those distorting mirrors at fairs. Man's made a beautifying mirror too in which he sees himself lovely and powerful and just and wise. It's his idea of himself.'" But when Smythe looks in the mirror, he sees a disfigured face. How could he possibly believe in a God who so cursed a child?

Bendrix struggles to place blame for the miserable turn his own story has taken: Sarah for suddenly leaving him (when he is usually the one to end affairs), Henry who couldn't "control his wife better," or the God dogma that people drag into everyday life. With the help of a private detective and Sarah's stolen diary, Bendrix learns that love *and* God have caused their separation: "She loves us both, I thought, but if there is to be a conflict between an image and a man, I know who will win. I could put my hand on her thigh or my mouth on her breast: he was imprisoned behind the altar and couldn't move to plead *his* cause." But Bendrix is wrong. Sarah sends him a letter, her last, while she's seriously ill with an apparent case of pneumonia: "'I love you but I can't see you again. I don't know how I'm going to live in this pain and longing and I'm praying to God all the time that he won't be hard on me, that he won't keep me alive.'"

And here's where Greene overindulges his own interest in Catholic abracadabra: He can't resist turning Sarah into a full-fledged bride of Christ in the Mary Magdalene tradition. Unable to dismiss the possibility that she's witnessed a miracle, Sarah gives up "ordinary, corrupt human love" and comes around to accepting Catholicism's "'whole bag of tricks'" before dying. Then she takes on saintly attributes with the revelation that Smythe's disfigured cheek clears after her kiss. Did she really appear as an angel to heal the mortally ill child who had earlier accompanied his private detective father to spy on her? And are we to believe that her vow really did raise Maurice from the dead?

Someone like me resists miracles being attributed to Sarah's intercession with God, finds the saintly gambit sentimental and instead gravitates to Bendrix as a companion in doubt. But then he becomes unreliable, swinging between love and hate in his grief and thinking perhaps he'll "ring up a doctor and ask him whether a faith cure is possible." Suddenly aware that his heart might *want* a miraculous Sarah, Bendrix attempts to end the whole affair with a prayer to the one in whom he doesn't believe: "O God, You've done enough, You've robbed me of enough, I'm too tired and old to learn to love, leave me alone for ever." *But isn't the wavering arc of recognition leaving him open for redemption?*

———

Like Maurice, cynicism often urges me to prefer coincidence or cause and effect over miracles. How about ripple effect, one thing tumbling after another in a chaotic universe? How about leaving God out of the equation and considering the power of dumb luck? I have a cat named Yuki and, to my knowledge, nobody prays for him—yet he's alive when he shouldn't be.

I should confess that I didn't like cats when, over a span of several years, I allowed my then young children to adopt three different kittens—because *they* liked them. This explains why nearly four years ago, when a now grown son phoned from Boston to say that one of his roommates was moving to San Francisco and could not take her cat Yuki along, and that pets are not allowed in his own new apartment, I had no problem saying: "Good luck finding someone who wants that fat (the fattest I'd ever seen) and cranky (the crankiest I'd ever seen) old cat. Who wants a rescued street fighter that snarls and hisses if things don't go his way, spits up hairballs, and sheds clumps of fur?" But as weeks passed, I occasionally asked (already knowing the answer) whether Yuki had a new home, and then (because my son loves him) gave in at the last possible moment. On a hot August day, after having helped clean cat fur and spit up from the Boston apartment, my husband and I drove toward Rochester with Yuki on the back seat.

My husband saw this turn of events with utter simplicity: Giving Yuki a home was the right thing to do. I remained relatively calm—acted like Lady Bountiful herself, except for a lot of eye-rolling—because I knew Yuki wouldn't last long. During the previous year, the three roommates had discovered several lumps amidst all Yuki's fat and fur, and a veterinarian supposedly diagnosed malignant tumors. Taking the terminal cat back to the apartment, they decided to make his last days his best days: In spite of limited funds, they switched from feeding him dry food to the aromatic delights of canned food.

After a few months of what should have been hospice care, the roommates noticed that Yuki's lumps were shrinking, and continued to shrink until they had completely disappeared. This development called for another visit to the vet, who told them what they already knew: The tumors were indeed gone. Thrilled by the news, the roommates (a Harvard-educated cell biologist among them) proclaimed that wet cat food cures cancer. I didn't buy this theory for a moment, and when I agreed to take Yuki, I expected that he would have a good death in the comfort of my home—soon.

After accepting that I serve only dry cat food, Yuki settled in and established aloof sovereignty over his new domain. Faded beach towels were quickly spread across upholstered furniture because he refused to stay off, and a plastic doorway gate was purchased to keep his food safe from Sophie, our middle-aged black Lab who's always ready for an extra meal. (Although, on the day they met, Yuki put the dog on notice with a surprisingly quick hind leg kick—his front paws having been declawed.) If Yuki wanted to go outside to snack on a little grass, he'd yowl at the back door and I'd let him out for a short ramble around the yard. Whenever I found the fattest of all cats sprawled on the deep window ledge in the kitchen, I knew he'd walked across the table to get there and I yelled empty threats. He'd simply turn away, sniff at the breeze coming through the screen—only to find it lacking, as if they just don't make breezes like they used to—and close his eyes. That was our arrangement for the first two years of cohabitation.

Then one October morning, Yuki didn't appear in the kitchen at breakfast time. My husband looked through the entire house, opening closet doors and checking dark crawl spaces. No Yuki. I joined the search and called his name all around the yard, looking under shrubbery and parked cars. No Yuki. We searched the garage, thinking he might have slipped inside and later found himself trapped. No Yuki. For twenty-eight days and nights, Yuki was missing, without a trace, and we didn't know how and when or why he had disappeared.

Two weeks before Thanksgiving, our daughter Nora returned from a year of living on Catalina Island, and she heard all about the end of Yuki—Dad's straightforward version, and Mom's mysterious, speculative one. She and I talked and cooked and watched movies together, and on Wednesday of the week before Thanksgiving, we were going shopping right after lunch. While I checked the stove, and the iron, and the locks, Nora went outside and was the first to see Yuki walking up the driveway toward the garage. I walked out the side door and found her crouched next to a gray cat. She said, "Yuki's home—I think."

He was little more than matted fur and bones, but Yuki was back. Nora carried him into the house and we tried to imagine where he'd been, why he'd never come to the door. He was so weak and listless that when she held him, stroking what already seemed like remains, she murmured, "I think Yuki's going to die." But he was hungry and we began an intensive care routine of feeding him a scant tablespoon of wet food several times a day. (Yes, wet food.) More than once I woke in the morning to tell my husband, "I think you should dig a deep hole behind the garage before the ground freezes." But Yuki didn't die, *wouldn't die*, and we kept feeding him wet food. I bought cans of light tuna because I thought he might like a treat now and then, and by mid-December, he seemed amazingly like a slim-built version of his old self. I called him our "Christmas Miracle."

The house was quiet while Yuki was away, and when he returned, I realized that I want him to live, and I want my son who loves him to know that I value one cat's life. For Mary and for all of us, I want Yuki to go on living—tumor survivor and walkabout warrior that he is—as proof that fate-apparent can be overcome. Yuki has his secrets, and I suspect there are remnants of vast, dark nights lurking behind his gaze. Choosing an assortment of brands and flavors of wet food isn't that much of a hardship; cleaning up clumps of wet and dry cat fur isn't all that time consuming.

———

Yuki is just now yowling for dinner (lamb and rice with gravy, these days), but I'm not ready to stop noticing the first signs of spring in the shy sunlight as I sit by his favorite window. I'm still wondering if Sarah Miles should have given more consideration to the impact of luck on our lives: Bad luck that Maurice was just there when the door was blown out, and good luck that he wasn't seriously injured. Or perhaps she should have learned that *every* day is a miracle, each time that she and Henry and Maurice rose to live another day was a miracle, not just the one time that Maurice rose from under the door. Perhaps what Greene was looking for while worrying miracles and luck is as simple as Maurice's discovery upon abandoning hate and choosing love: "I thought to myself: I remember. This is what hope feels like."

I'm not finished noticing that my world has turned rather smoothly for the past few weeks. I'm pleased that my mother was happy during a recent Easter visit, and that she enjoyed shopping for a new pair of shoes and selecting yarn with which to crochet another afghan. I'm pleased that Mary felt well enough to board a plane for a vacation in Florida this morning. And I knock on wood while reviewing the whereabouts of my children, pleased that everyone seems busy with work or study, pleased that nobody seems on the brink of crisis, and content that they seldom want or need my advice.

I'm not finished remembering that Easter Sunday dawned without chocolate eggs, marshmallow chicks, and jelly beans because none of the children were home. But my husband, mother, and I had our morning coffee and drove off to attend an early church service; that way, my husband could work at the hospital for a few hours, I could bake a piecrust, and Mom could clean the asparagus well before our neighbors arrived for dinner. My husband dropped Mom and I at the front door so she wouldn't have far to walk, and he went off to find parking. Once inside the church, we sat behind a friend I've known since college, exchanged hellos, and waited for my husband to join us.

Finally, the organ began playing alleluia music to announce the joyful procession of priests and choir: This is the church celebration of resurrection, of victory over death. I watched the parade, smiled at various children sitting near us, admired their new Easter outfits, and noticed the sexy black shoes that the woman across the aisle was wearing, without stockings. *I wonder what time I should put the ham in the oven. Maybe I should microwave the sweet potatoes for a few minutes so they don't take so long. I'll put the banana cream pie together last.* I lip-synched the words to a Psalm and recited a creed. We sat, kneeled, stood, sat, kneeled, stood and exchanged hand clasps and cheek kisses during the congregation's offering of peace. And then the Eucharistic rites began, and there I was sitting between my husband and my mother with the organ music gaining force and sailing off into eternity and the voices in the choir swelling and filling the high-peaked ceiling with words of hope and a promise that if I believe in Him then He would raise me up on the last day and there between my husband and mother I began to tremble, when I thought I'd come for them.

After the Falling

"Times like these, the family is necessary. Don't you think?
Be together, stay together? This is how we live through
the things that scare us half to death."
—Don DeLillo, *Falling Man*

I need to remember when "I love you" became the closer for every family phone call. My oldest son who worked for the Red Cross in a Maryland suburb of Washington, D.C. spoke those words when he called to assure me of his safety after terrorists crashed an airplane into the Pentagon during their multi-target jihad. Before that day, mother, father, and four young adult children had mostly been casual about their declarations of affection, assuming that one phone conversation would be followed by another, that our voices would magically pulse from here to there through clear skies or stormy weather, that we would have each other tomorrow. The morning of the planes tainted everything with uncertainty, even little things, and saying "I love you" felt suddenly important. Then, over time, I began saying the words as if by rote, treating the vow as if it had always been part of family custom. The distilled moment of the closer's inception returned when Don DeLillo's 2007 novel *Falling Man* pressed against my knowing of September 11, 2001.

Sandra Swinburne

Tuesday Morning, in the Name of Islam

Flight 11 struck the north tower of the World Trade Center at 8:46, followed by Flight 175 striking the south tower at 9:02. Then Flight 77 hit the Pentagon at 9:37, and Flight 93, presumed to be targeting a Washington, D. C. destination, crashed into a Pennsylvania field at 10:03 after passengers fought back. The south tower collapsed at 9:59 followed by the north tower at 10:28, crushing nearby buildings in the wake of their ruin. Many likened the death-filled landscape in lower Manhattan to a nightmare vision of nuclear winter.

Where Were You?

In fictional time and space, DeLillo's Keith Neudecker is talking on the phone in his World Trade Center office when a blast knocks him from his chair. He feels "the tower lurching," sees "the ceiling begin to ripple," and notices a "stink of something familiar." A character named Benny T. later admits to his East Harlem Alzheimer's support group: "'I was on the crapper. I hated myself later. People said where were you when it happened. I didn't tell them where I was.'"

An easy hour and a quarter plane trip away through real time and space, I was standing under a tree in suburban Rochester, New York with three men from Irondequoit Gutters and Home Improvements. I noticed how young they were; I noticed an American flag painted across the door of their truck, its edges rippled to give the effect that it was blowing in the wind. We reviewed the plan for replacement of the worn-out copper eaves trough on my house, they raised their ladders, and I returned to the kitchen where I sat at the table studying an anthology of English Romantic writers for a graduate school course I was taking. That's what I was doing when the terrorists struck.

The Last Good Obsession

In Medias Res

But DeLillo does not begin at the beginning; he introduces Keith, Manhattan's discontented Everyman turned fallen angel, as he steps out of the burning tower and into the far reaches of hell on earth:

> It was not a street anymore but a world, a time and space of falling ash and near night. He was walking north through rubble and mud and there were people running past holding towels to their faces or jackets over their heads. They had handkerchiefs pressed to their mouths. They had shoes in their hands, a woman with a shoe in each hand, running past him. They ran and fell, some of them, confused and ungainly, with debris coming down around them, and there were people taking shelter under cars.

Keith passes remnants of yesterday—office papers fluttering through the air and a sign advertising "a Breakfast Special"—but today means "a man seated on the sidewalk coughing up blood," and "figures in windows a thousand feet up, dropping into free space." He walks away from "all those writhing lives back there," hears "the sound of the second fall . . . the north tower coming down," and keeps going. Yet he cannot escape his own damaged inner world, already fragmented long before this: "That was him coming down, the north tower."

Keith makes his way through city streets wearing a coat of blood, ash, and "pulverized matter," with glass splinters implanted and glistening from areas of exposed skin. Some of the blood and bits of "matter" belong to Rumsey, a friend with an office down the hall whom he tried to save but couldn't. When an electrician in a service truck offers him a ride, he gives his wife Lianne's address, even though they've been separated for a year and a half. On a day when the world just might be ending, thirty-nine-year-old Keith suddenly recognizes "where he'd been going all along." He wants the only connections he knows as home; he wants to be with Lianne and their eight-year-old son Justin.

Meanwhile

I had made little progress with the Romantics when the bell at the side entrance rang and I opened the door to the workers pacing around in the driveway. Rick, the owner of the aluminum gutter business, asked whether I was watching TV, and I was taken aback by the question. Why would he care? I told him that I was reading and felt silently uncomfortable with his interest in what I was doing. Then he began to explain that one of his employees had just heard something crazy on the radio. Something about a plane in New York City crashing into a tower. I forgot about my flash of annoyance and invited the three men inside to the television room where I fumbled with the remote control to get at the news—only to find the reports unfathomable.

What were we seeing and hearing? A first plane. A second plane. Two towers, two different planes? Over and over, we watched a plane fly into a tower. What could explain this? One of the men had a relative in Brooklyn, so he called him on his cell phone to ask what he knew, which was no more than we knew. The four of us watched and talked and speculated about airplanes zeroing in on buildings like bombs. After maybe ten minutes of that, strange as it now seems, the men muttered among themselves and agreed that they might as well get back to tearing off the old gutters. I walked them to the door and told them to come back if they wanted to check for news updates.

During that early phase of processing the reports, my husband called from the hospital where he works and we spoke of the horror. He said that doctors, nurses, and administrators were organizing for the possibility that, since there were so many people in the targeted buildings, victims might be transported upstate to major medical centers. Or hospital personnel with trauma care skills might be needed in Manhattan. I said things like, "It's so awful," and he asked if I'd heard from our then twenty-six-year-old son Mathew. I questioned why he thought about hearing from that particular child since neither he nor any of our other children were in New York at the time. When he explained that he'd like to know there hadn't been any Red Cross meetings near the Pentagon when the plane hit, I thought he had things mixed up. "No, no," I said. "The planes crashed in New York." He countered that he'd just seen a news report in a patient's room and a passenger plane had also crashed into the Pentagon. I still didn't believe him and asked whether he was certain he had the facts right; he insisted that he did. How had I missed that bulletin? Had the departure of the workers coincided with the breaking news? I needed to get back to the television.

Although chances were slight, I began to worry (in the obsessive way that I tend to worry) about the possibility that Mathew could have been in the vicinity of the third crash. Even a tiny glimpse of personal involvement changes how my nerve fibers respond to catastrophe, makes them raw and ready to feed the dark side of my imagination. I saw my child (*"my child" no matter how old*) driving on a street near the Pentagon, walking on a sidewalk toward the Pentagon, sitting at a table inside the Pentagon. And I saw gleaming planes aimed at the Pentagon. I dialed his cell phone number and left a message of feigned calm—"Just wanted to check in with you"—when he didn't pick up. Then the doorbell rang; having heard on the radio that there was ever-worsening news, the gutter crew wanted to rejoin me in front of the television.

We four sat on the edges of the battered sofa and chairs for the next few hours. On an ordinary day, I would have pushed sodas and snacks on young visitors in my house, insisting that they have something even if they claimed not to want anything. But there was no hospitality that day; all eyes were fixed on the screen, each of us hoping to see something that would explain what was happening. As we

watched, one of the men asked, "Did anyone else just see a body falling down from the tower?" None of us could answer, but we studied
the images that followed with heightened acuity and began to comprehend that people trapped inside were jumping.

Sometime during my bug-eyed response to televised havoc I was
startled by the ringing phone, but slumped in relief when I heard
Mathew tell me that he was fine. I again mumbled stock phrases that
did not touch the magnitude of what was going on in the world and he
explained that he would be among those providing support services
for emergency workers at the Pentagon crash site in the days ahead.
He sounded preoccupied and said that he had to go, but he deliberately added, "I love you," to which I replied, "I love you, too." We
were scared; we meant what we said.

Next

Lianne takes Keith for emergency medical care, and then, in spite
of their past unhappiness together, "the eventual extended grimness
called their marriage," she takes him back into her bed and her life
without mention of needs and desires, and without vows to try again
at love. Keith tells her that he's not only there because his own apartment is too close to the carnage: "'It was more than that.'" Lianne
manages their togetherness by undertaking a sort of "guardianship
of the survivor," and even though she does not tell Keith, it's more
than that: "She wanted him here, nearby, but felt no edge of self-
contradiction or self-denial. Just waiting, that was all, a broad pause in
recognition of a thousand sour days and nights, not so easily set aside.
The matter needed time."

Thirty-eight-year-old Lianne cares for Justin, checks up on her
aging mother, works as a freelance editor, facilitates a writing group
for Alzheimer's patients, and obsesses over her own thought pro-
cesses. Fear of developing Alzheimer's disease, the illness that, years
ago, precipitated her father's decision to commit suicide rather than

live with a crumbling mind, casts a shadow over her life and seems to distract her from full emotional engagement in relationships. So Lianne typically watches and waits at the perimeters rather than initiate acts of living, tendencies substantiated by her mother's theory that she had married Keith in a deluded attempt to recapture her father, to experience feeling "'dangerously alive'" as a way of being, while in her motherly opinion, Keith was only "'built for weekends.'"

Lianne's own maternal behavior reveals another layer of her distant nature. She does not know that her son takes binoculars to his best friends' house so the three of them can search the sky for more airplanes sent by "Bill Lawton," their naive rendition of "bin Laden." When her mother asks about Justin's response to Keith's return home, Lianne avoids the heart of the matter: "'The kid is fine. Who knows how the kid is? He's fine, he's back in school.'" Rather than worry over her boy's emotional adjustments, she drifts back to the hours when she feared Keith was buried in the rubble, and media images of the falling towers resurface in her thoughts. Then she gazes at two still life paintings—"*[n]atura morta*"—searching to explain a certain unreachable, unknowable depth that is not unlike her own, "something in the brushstrokes that held a mystery she could not name, or in the irregular edges of vases and jars, some reconnoiter inward, human and obscure, away from the very light and color of the paintings."

In Search of Meaning

The morning after the planes struck, I woke to a brilliant blue sky, I mean dazzling blue, and the sun sparkled through the east windows next to my bed. I lay wondering if perhaps my mind was not right; perhaps yesterday did not happen as I seemed to remember. Otherwise, how could the sun rise?

I picked through the jumble in my head and tried to reconstruct the previous twenty-four hours. I couldn't comprehend the tireless planning and nurturing of belief and hate required to execute the attacks that I had seen on television. I couldn't comprehend the numbers of ordinary people who were either pronounced or presumed dead because they went to work. If the horrors of yesterday really happened, how could the sun rise today? I wanted to know: How could the sun rise? My mind flipped to an association with *The Sun Also Rises*, and I felt a little ashamed of allowing the title of a novel into space that should be filled with mourning the dead. My thoughts skittered into wordplay and I began to interrogate *also*. The sun rises in addition to what? The sun and what else? Or perhaps the sun falls but rises as well? Falls at night, yet rises come morning. I wondered if Hemingway took his title from a meaningful source, so I got up and did a computer search which directed me to Ecclesiastes 1.4-9:

> 4 *One* generation passeth away, and *another* generation cometh: but the earth abideth for ever.

> 5 The sun also ariseth, and the sun goeth down, and hasteth to his place where he arose.

> 6 The wind goeth toward the south, and turneth about unto the north; it whirleth about continually, and the wind returneth again according to his circuits.

> 7 All the rivers run into the sea; yet the sea *is* not full; unto the place from whence the rivers come, thither they return again.

> 8 All things *are* full of labour; man cannot utter *it*: the eye is not satisfied with seeing, nor the ear filled with hearing.

The Last Good Obsession

9 The thing that hath been, it *is that* which shall be; and that which is done *is* that which shall be done: and *there is* no new *thing* under the sun.

Nothing new under the sun. What had risen, in addition to the sun, was yet more mass killing of innocents—even though the world must surely be weary from such repetitions. *The Holocaust. Hiroshima.* But the 9/11 death delivery system seemed particularly insidious in that some of the victims were trapped inside the planes, forced to be part of the jet-fueled bombs. No, even the cruel impulse behind that wasn't new.

But there was more that bothered me. Not only had the sun and the wind and the waters continued on their paths during that first new day after the planes, but my eyes remained dry. Furthermore, I had every intention of returning to the solipsism of the English Romantics by mid-morning. How could I see yesterday, yet not weep? Surely I had been given—the world had been given—a job for tears. Shouldn't grief be *enacted* by every witness to this human failure to love life? I found myself lacking and wished for experience with a Wailing Wall tradition. Perhaps if I had been taught how to mourn publicly . . . . Would that have prepared my tear ducts for these times? Perhaps from acts of mourning one comes to feel the reality of those losses that are apart from the immediate personal sphere.

Sick of my own thoughts, I went downstairs, made a pot of coffee, and flipped on the television to catch up on the news. Re-entering the spool of broadcast images, I tried to force myself into knowing and feeling, tried to will my thoughts to tears, but I could not make the plane flying into the tower a real plane that made me cry out in horror. Every image seemed impossible. Reports continued to show clips that looked not unlike the video game screens that had flashed in that same room under the command of gangly boys who flicked control buttons with their thumbs. *But these planes are real and the people are real. This is real, this is real.* Confused and tearless, I drank coffee and waited for the gutter workers to arrive before settling down with my books.

Considering Tomorrows

Keith faces the problems of how to live after being a witness to so much breaking and burning and death. He begins to notice changes in his own patterns of consciousness: "He used to want to fly out of self-awareness, day and night, a body in raw motion. Now he finds himself drifting into spells of reflection, thinking not in clear units, hard and linked, but only absorbing what comes, drawing things out of time and memory and into some dim space that bears his collected experience."

Having seen pandemonium roar through the world and wrest loved ones from their families, Keith knows that he should focus on mending his own relationships. He walks Justin to school and plays catch with him, and he sleeps next to Lianne until he's ready to make love to her again. But he also begins a secret affair with Florence, a fellow-survivor whose briefcase he carried out of the tower, because something even more compelling than sex draws them together: They had each been inside one of the doomed towers, yet had walked out. When she tells of remembering smoke and firemen and "some people in the rubble, all that steel and glass, just injured people sitting dreaming, they were like dreamers bleeding," Keith listens. When she starts over again, he listens again, "noting every detail, trying to find himself in the crowd."

For Lianne, maintaining control is a way of life—except when she snaps and takes out her anger and fear on a Middle Eastern woman who lives in the same apartment building. She lies awake next to Keith, not knowing if he can ever be truly present in their marriage, but wanting him just the same. She watches and waits, enduring the silence and secrets in her marriage. With a mind that's ever-spinning, she fills her head with all the news she can find about the attacks, dissects her own suspect memory, recreates her father's sensibility, and contemplates the struggles of those in her Alzheimer's writing group.

With their failing minds, Benny T., Omar H., Carmen G., Eugene A., and Rosellen respond to the tumult around them in bursts of emotion-filled language. Some write that the devil is responsible for all hell being unleashed on earth, and they wonder: "How could God let this happen? Where was God when this happened?" Others feel closer to God, believing that he has a plan. And there are those, like me, who cannot process what happened: "'You're looking right at it. But it's not really happening.'"

Keith and Lianne see endless grieving over lost loved ones all around them, but given a second chance, they are still unable to access and articulate their own feelings in ways that can build emotional intimacy. Although Keith ends his affair and means to stay in his marriage, he eventually finds himself wanting to escape from the daily needs and attachments of family life. He enters the world of professional poker tournaments where he believes he can control outcomes as an "agent of free choice." Presenting himself as a loner with ice in his veins, he's determined to defeat the uncertainties of chance by sticking with the concrete: "He wasn't playing for the money. He was playing for the chips." In the very game that he used to play with his friend Rumsey, Keith believes that from here on out, he can beat his adversaries without suffering any "major loss." Yet when he goes home to Lianne and Justin, he is at a loss for words: "There was no language, it seemed, to tell them how he spent his days and nights."

Lianne guards against loss in her own ways. She stops socializing with friends, although she misses "the comical midlife monologues of the clinically self-absorbed," in part because people are uncomfortable around Keith. So she waits for him, and theirs are erotic reunions when he returns home from tournaments, but her emotions are in check. Life has taught her that "'there are some men who are only half here. Let's not say men. Let's say people.'" Lianne knows in her head that such half-presence provides safety for the vulnerable self, but allowing her heart a voice, she urges Keith to always come back home, "'with the idea that we're permanent.'" In spite of having made that plea, having put those words out into the world, she finds that over time, she can "be alone, in reliable calm, she and the kid, the way they were before the planes appeared that day, silver crossing blue."

Shake Me

Falling Man is about personal failures, *our* personal failures. DeLillo could have written an expansive political novel about 9/11, but instead he chose to probe the human flaw, a sort of non-physiologic Alzheimer's, that lets us disconnect and forget even when we should most be remembering. He delivers a cautionary tale about the state of the human psyche, about an epidemic estrangement from each other which can become political when manipulated with ideology. He sees horror as the end result of failure to love life: "This was the world now."

I re-read *Falling Man* as an antidote for my own emotional drowsiness. No longer pursuing plot, I wanted to be shaken by the performance artist called Falling Man—"Heartless Exhibitionist or Brave New Chronicler of the Age of Terror"—who simulates the death spirals of those who jumped from the burning towers with the eventual plan of ending his own life during a final spectacle. Lianne and I are unnerved when we come upon preparations for a Falling Man performance. We see him high above the ground on a railway maintenance platform, he fastens his harness, and waits for a passenger train to emerge from a tunnel: "There would be those aboard who see him standing and those who see him jump, all jarred out of their reveries or their newspapers or muttering stunned into their cell phones. These people had not seen him attach the safety harness. They would only see him fall out of sight." *Shocked into remembering.*

The Last Good Obsession

And I wanted another encounter with the final ten page jolt where DeLillo *means* to shock me into imagining what happened inside the towers. I watch Hammad, a young terrorist aboard Flight 11, struggling to control his own mind while preparing for the imminent crash and eternal life: "Forget the world. Be unmindful of the thing called the world." He buckles his seatbelt and watches a water bottle fall from a counter and roll in the aisle just before "the aircraft struck the tower, heat, then fuel, then fire, and a blast wave passed through the structure that sent Keith Neudecker out of his chair and into a wall." Under an illusionist's spell, I believe I'm flying into death with Hammad only to find myself falling to the floor with Keith.

Inside a chamber of horror: "When the tower swung finally back to vertical he pushed himself off the floor and moved to the doorway. The ceiling at the far end of the hall moaned and opened. The stress was audible and then it opened, objects coming down, panels and wallboard. Plaster dust filled the area and there were voices along the hall." Keith finds his friend Rumsey unconscious; his head split open to reveal the soft center, but still breathing. *DeLillo means to batter my heart.* While trying to move him, he glances outside and sees the unforgettable, "an instant of something sideways, going past the window, white shirt, hand up, falling before he saw it." A man from an upper floor had jumped to escape death by fire. Keith struggles to lift and carry his friend until he hears him "gasp" into open-eyed death: "The whole business of being Rumsey was in shambles now."

But, then again, I wanted my second reading of *Falling Man* to have a different ending: Keith and Lianne would be so shaken by the surrounding deathscape that they would feel miraculously alive and try harder to find happiness together. The stillness that encases their emotions would crackle and fall away; they would remember and learn and rewrite the future. Keith would not become (as he fears) "a self-operating mechanism, like a humanoid robot that understands two hundred voice commands, far-seeing, touch-sensitive but totally, rigidly controllable." Lianne would not withdraw "calmly, in control" as she fades into her own still life existence. I wanted that new ending for them because many of us need a new ending. After the fires of 9/11 stopped smoldering and most of the body parts had been collected, many of us returned to petty concerns and self-absorption; we stopped paying attention to things that matter.

From a Distance

I had watched the aftershocks of the terrorist attacks, and I had heard about some firsthand experiences of Red Cross workers who implemented support services set up at the Pentagon crash site. Carried back to those days, this is the one I remember: While passing out bottled water, my son's friend noticed a young man dressed in white coveralls sitting on a knoll, apart from everyone else. Because he looked so isolated, she went over to offer him water, talk with him, ask him about his job. The boy—*I'm going to call him a boy because she told me that he appeared to be around twenty years old*—explained that he waits with a bag until recovery workers signal him. Once summoned, he goes into the rubble and picks up body parts and places them in the bag for identification.

During the spring of 2003, I was talking with a friend in front of my house when a pickup truck slowed at the driveway. I noticed the billows of an American flag painted across the truck's door and then saw the driver, the young contractor with whom I had shared early news of 9/11, framed by the open window. I was surprised at how happy I was to see him, and I greeted him in a voice that might ordinarily be reserved for a long-lost friend. I walked to the truck and asked the expected: How are you? How's business? We small-talked until he could say: "I thought about calling you on the one year anniversary of 9/11 but my wife said it was weird." I wanted that young man to drag me back to that horrible day because I needed dragging back, and I told him I wished he had called, that we should never forget, but even as I talked about remembering, I was forgetting.

The Last Good Obsession

Up Close

Falling Man kept creeping through my mind long after the actual reading stopped. *What drives Keith? What drives Lianne? What drives me?* I wrote about them and about me to remember, yet became lost in fears and failures as I studied my own still nature. Being conscious of an inclination toward "the clinically self-absorbed," I might have ended these analytic efforts after raising the young contractor's unmade phone call (and there I am forgetting). But circumstances can change in an instant; a different ending can demand space on the page. I know this because on the dazzling September morning that was yesterday, a young man, not our child yet close in age to our oldest, lay dead beneath a rock cliff while my husband and I hiked nearby. He had plunged from a mountain ledge, sixty feet of falling, falling.

On our last day of vacation, we woke to a dazzling blue sky. After eating too many waffles with too much syrup, we entered a perfectly beautiful outdoor world, perfect for hiking with temperatures around seventy degrees and a breeze that carried the silken breath of a nearby mountain lake. Rambling downhill and into the spicy scent of hemlock trees, we were scarcely away from the sounds of road traffic when we spotted four deer grazing among ferns. They looked up only briefly to notice us, and we commented on their tameness. But I couldn't linger; I had bears on my mind. I'd heard that a mother and two cubs were seen scavenging around a cottage up the road and I wanted to see them, having only seen bears in zoos or from a distance at a town dump in the Adirondacks. So intent was I to see black bears that I failed to see a little spotted snake coiled on the trail and hopped sideways only at the last moment when my husband yelled, "Look out."

We have vacationed in the Shawangunk Mountains with our children for the past twenty-two summers. Intent on modeling a spirit of adventure, each year we looked for new options among the trails, boulder fields, crevices, lakes, and caves; but since I am afraid of heights, I worried incessantly about the children falling, and in the past, the youngest often pleaded with me not to squeeze so tightly when I grabbed a small hand. For myself, a silent chant of *don't look down, don't look down* carried me through places I hadn't believed myself capable of going. Only in the past few years have my husband and I begun to accept our retirement from rough terrain because depth perception and balance now play tricks on us. Falling twice on easy paths during this summer's visit, first on a wet rock and next on a tree root across an uphill trail, was proof enough for me that I belong on relatively flat, solid ground.

While all four children were with us during the last days of August, they decided to hire a guide to take them on some world-class rock climbs. They were looking for thrills, looking to push themselves into feeling "dangerously alive" while roped and harnessed against sheer rock face. We didn't discourage them and we didn't go watch, couldn't bear to watch; when they returned late in the afternoon, still high on adrenaline, we were relieved and happy to see them. Mathew, nearly thirty-two, admitted to being scared out of his mind while clinging to the lip of a towering cliff. Ian, our twenty-eight-year-old second child, claimed with a grin that he had experienced a state of higher consciousness in which he saw God four times. Nora, twenty-six and increasingly daring, climbed with a stress fracture in her foot but found mountain euphoria worth the pain. Alec, twenty-three and accustomed to playing up from his place in the birth order, was ready to go again. So two days later, after Mathew had departed to begin another year of grad school, the others hired a guide for a full day of harder, higher climbs. Everyone returned—although two hours later than expected—sweaty and safe.

One by one, each of our children returned to Baltimore or Philadelphia or Boston or San Francisco and to a life that is physically separate from the family we once were. My husband and I were on our own the last few days of vacation, so each morning we hiked seven or eight miles on easy terrain; afterwards, we'd go to the lake looking for its icy shock to revive us. One particularly chilly day, we stood together on the dock—a bearded man wearing baggy plaid trunks and a slouched, henna-haired woman in a prim, navy-and-white-flowered-skirt-style swimsuit. I hesitated and talked about how cold the lake looked, curled my toes and gazed at the water as I usually do, until finally I reached for my husband's hand and insisted that we jump together on the count of three, like two children.

Yes, we were swaddled in well-being during those last days in the mountains. On the morning of our farewell hike, my husband looked rested, and I felt more alive, more engaged with the world than when I'd arrived. We each spoke of feeling happy that our children had been together, we gave directions to a pair of lost joggers, and I kept up my bear watch. But minutes after I hopped to avoid a spotted snake, my husband was asked to help at an accident scene in an area of dizzying ledges and fallen boulders. He climbed over some of the very same rock fields that we had judged beyond our diminished abilities, and when he reached a young man lying at the base of a cliff, all he could do was pronounce death. Then the rescue crews and police arrived and began swarming the area; finding no actual witness, the next move was to interrogate verbs: *fall* or *jump*.

While we drove home, I was fixated on needing to hear the voices of our children and know they were safe. I used my cell phone to dial and re-dial until I had asked each child what he or she was doing, and had told of our recent hikes, the bears that we did not see, and the young man's death. Four separate times I said "I love you," and I heard those words spoken in return. Yet while I was talking on the phone, or perhaps while taking my turn driving, a young man's parents were contacted by the police and told that their son had died from injuries sustained in a fall on a mountain; they were told that a police investigation was underway. *Their boy, even though in years he was a young man, for all yesterdays and all tomorrows, their boy. Falling, falling.*

My husband was quiet as we sped across the New York State Thruway; he said that he did not want to talk about the death he had seen that morning. I said things like, I know and I'm sorry, sorry for everyone. But I didn't know; I hadn't climbed over boulders and squeezed through crevices and hadn't seen the boy in shambles.

When we reached home, Sophie the dog and Yuki the cat were glad to see us. We unpacked the car and shuffled through the piles of mail that covered the kitchen table. We split a can of beef barley soup and nearly finished a box of crackers and a square of yellow cheese. I checked my e-mail while my husband went to the store for cereal and milk. Ordinary things; we did ordinary things until we were tired. And then we climbed into our bed where we lay side by side in the dark.

He said that he'd never seen anything like the boy's death and he reached over to take my hand. We each murmured "I love you." I could think of nothing else to say, not then. But in my stillness, I planned that one day soon I would tell my husband that he is a good man and thank him for working so hard to care for so many, for making a family with me, and for sharing the complicated story that comes with twining lives together. I reminded myself that this wasn't the first time I'd encountered epiphany, either from life or from fiction, but I should try again to say other things that need saying, things that are buried during a thirty-five year marriage, yet remain unquiet. Those feelings of discontent and loneliness that I sometimes believe are special to me alone, but in truth I see in others all around me—I should talk to him about those. And then I thought about being alive, about second chances, and lost chances as we waited for sleep to carry us through the night.

Readings and Notes

Abrams, M. H. "New Criticism." *A Glossary of Literary Terms*. 7th ed. Fort Worth: Harcourt, 1999.

Birkerts, Sven. *Readings*. Saint Paul: Graywolf, 1999.

Bloom, Harold. *How to Read and Why*. New York: Scribner, 2000.

Brown, Norman O. *Love's Body*. Berkley: U of California P, 1966.

Dabkowski, Colin. "The Palace Burlesque, Uncovered." *Buffalo News* 28 Oct. 2007. 30 Oct. 2007 <http://www.buffalonews.com/entertainment/story/194150.html>.

Dart, John. *The Laughing Savior*. New York: Harper, 1976.

DeLillo, Don. *Falling Man*. New York: Scribner, 2007.

Donohue, Michael. "Russell and Mary." Reading Sponsored by *Georgia Review*. Mo Pitkin's House of Satisfaction, New York. 03 May 2007.

Faulkner, William. *As I Lay Dying*. 1930. Corrected Text. New York: Vintage International, 1990.

—. "The Bear." *Go Down, Moses*. 181-315.

—. "The Fire and the Hearth." *Go Down, Moses*. 33-95.

—. *Go Down, Moses*. 1942. New York: Vintage International, 1990.

—. *The Hamlet*. 1931. Corrected Text. New York: Vintage International, 1991.

—. *Light in August*. 1932. Corrected Text. New York: Vintage International, 1990.

—. "Old People." *Go Down, Moses*. 157-180.

—. *The Unvanquished.* 1934. Corrected Text. New York: Vintage International, 1991.

Flaubert, Gustave. *Madame Bovary.* 1857. Ed. and trans. Paul de Man. Trans. Eleanor Marx Aveling. Critical ed. New York: Norton, 1965.

Freudenheim, Nina. Interview. "The Palace Burlesque, Uncovered." Dabkowski.

Goethe, Johann Wolfgang von. *The Sorrows of Young Werther and Selected Writings.* 1774. Trans. Catherine Hutter. New York: Signet, 1962.

Greene, Graham. *The End of the Affair.* 1951. London: Penguin, 1975.

Hockney, David. Interview. "True to Life: David Hockney's Photocollages." Weschler 319-52.

The Holy Bible: Authorized King James Version. New York: Oxford UP, n.d.

James, Henry. *Washington Square.* 1881. New York: Modern Lib., 2002.

Kundera, Milan. *Identity.* Trans. Linda Asher. New York: HarperPerennial, 1998.

Laing, R. D. *The Divided Self.* London: Penguin, 1990.

Lawrence, D. H. *Studies in Classical American Literature.* 1923. London: Penguin, 1977.

—. *Women in Love.* 1920. New York: Modern Lib., 1949.

Maclean, Norman. *A River Runs Through It and Other Stories.* Chicago: U of Chicago P, 1976.

McGuinness, Frank. *There Came a Gypsy Riding.* London: Faber, 2007.

Morrison, Toni. *Beloved.* 1987. New York: Plume, 1988.

Nabokov, Vladimir. *Lolita.* 1955. New York: Vintage International, 1989.

—. *Speak Memory: An Autobiography Revisited.* 1951. New York: Vintage International, 1989.

Paglia, Camille. *Break, Blow, Burn.* New York: Pantheon, 2005.

—. *Sexual Personae: Art and Decadence from Nefertiti to Emily Dickinson.* 1990. New York: Vintage, 1991.

Pynchon, Thomas. *The Crying of Lot 49*. 1965. New York: Perrennial Classics, 1999.

Richards, I. A. *Practical Criticism: A Study of Literary Judgment*. New York: Harcourt, 1929.

Rilke, Rainer Maria. *Letters to a Young Poet*. 1903-1908. Trans. Joan M. Burnham. Novato, CA: New World, 2000.

Rinpoche, Sogyal. *The Tibetan Book of Living and Dying*. Ed. Patrick Gaffney and Andrew Harvey. San Francisco: Harper, 1992.

Scarry, Elaine. *On Beauty and Being Just*. Princeton: Princeton UP, 1999.

Shakespeare, William. *Antony and Cleopatra*. *The Complete Works of Shakespeare*. Ed. David Bevington. 4th ed. New York: Longman-Addison, 1997. 1293-1344.

Sophocles. "Oedipus Rex." *The Oedipus Cycle*. Trans. Dudley Fitts and Robert Fitzgerald. San Diego: Harvest/Harcourt, 1977.

Spencer, Charles. "Tears of Embarrassment." Rev. of *There Came a Gypsy Riding*, by Frank McGuinness. *Daily Telegraph* [London] 20 Jan. 2007:A19.

Swift, Graham. *Last Orders*. New York: Vintage International, 1997.

"The Tease: Burlesque Performers from the 1950s & 60s." Robert and Nina Freudenheim Collection. George Eastman House, Rochester, New York.

Turgenev, Ivan Sergeyevich. *Prayer. Familiar Quotations*. Ed. John Bartlett. 14th ed. Boston: Little Brown, 1968.

"Were Critics on Board for Frank McGuiness' *Riding*?" *Theatre.com* 28 Jan. 2007. 28 Jan. 2007 <http://www.theatre.com/buzz/ buzz_story_print.aspx?id=3005576>.

Weschler, Lawrence. *Vermeer in Bosnia: A Reader*. New York: Pantheon, 2004.

Zeigler, Michael. "'Predator' Given 16 Years in Prison." *Democrat and Chronicle* [Rochester, NY] 25 Oct. 2007: A1.

The Author

Sandra Swinburne was a neonatal intensive care nurse and later a stay-at-home mother before returning to college to study literature. She published a critical essay based on her master's degree research, "Lilith in Mississippi: Reading Mythic Desire in *If I Forget Thee, Jerusalem,*" in *Mississippi Quarterly: The Journal of Southern Cultures.* The tempting possibilities found in creative/critical writing resulted in "Essay, Dresses, and Fish," published in *Short Takes: Brief Encounters with Contemporary Nonfiction,* Ed. Judith Kitchen. *The Last Good Obsession: Thoughts on Finding Life in Fiction* is her first book, an out-growth of her MFA thesis submitted to Rainier Writing Workshop at Pacific Lutheran University in 2008. Swinburne lives with her husband in Pittsford, New York.

OVENBIRD

Judith Kitchen's Ovenbird Books promotes innovative, imaginative, experimental works of creative nonfiction.

Ovenbird Books
The Circus Train by Judith Kitchen

Judith Kitchen Select:
The Slow Farm by Tarn Wilson
The Last Good Obsession by Sandra Swinburne
Dear Boy, An Epistolary Memoir by Heather Weber

www.ovenbirdbooks.org